The Politics of Loving God

Courageous Truths for
Contentious Times

—ഝ—

David Fowler

The Politics of Loving God
By David Fowler

Printed in the United States of America

ISBN 978-1493562855

Endorsements

—ᴠ—

David Fowler's book, "The Politics of Loving God," is a must read for all pastors and church officers. It will challenge you with the rights we have as American citizens and the responsibilities we have as Christian leaders. It will equip you to address the Culture of Politics with the Truth of the Gospel.

Dr. Wilson Benton
Pastor Emeritus, Kirk of the Hills, St. Louis,
and former adjunct and visiting professor,
Covenant Theological Seminary

At a time in history when it's easier to ignore important issues or attack those who represent them, David Fowler provides a thought-filled guide for those who desire to make a difference. Laced with seasoned wisdom and real-life examples, "The Politics of Loving God" enables disciples of Jesus to not flinch in regard to the truth while genuinely learning how to love one's neighbor as oneself.

Dave Buehring
Executive Director, Lionshare
Franklin, Tennessee

Finally an intellectual debate that removes issues from the often pejorative name calling, to true Biblical honesty. Should be extremely helpful to any serious Pastor seeking to be culturally relevant in this post-Christian 21st Century.

Bill Darnell, D.Min.

How can we be "A Nation Under God" if the people of God are not engaged, and leading in authority, duty and wisdom? David amazingly reminds us in this book of our calling and the consequence of our apathy and absence from the front lines of a battle for keeps: a battle for our time and all time!

Michael DelGiorno
WTN Nashville

David Fowler is involved, informed, insightful, and inspirational, and his book is a reflection of that.

Mitch McClure, MACM
Pastor, Middle Valley Church of God

Every serious-minded Christian ought to read and study this book! It provides the Biblical basis for Christian involvement in the political process. David Fowler rightly argues that there is a direct relationship between loving God, loving man, and engaging the political process. Small groups of Christians could profit by studying this book together.

Dr. Charles McGowan
Pastor Emeritus, Christ Presbyterian Church,
Brentwood, TN

Highly readable and profoundly persuasive, especially for those who believe Christians should steer clear of controversies. Everything David Fowler says he has lived and learned.

Tom Minnery
Senior Vice President, Focus on the Family

We are repeatedly reminded that we should "love God and love our neighbor", but my dear friend David Fowler, brings an entirely new dimension to that admonition. What does that term really mean when we get to the intersection of the truth of God's Word and the political realities of our day? How do we both understand and apply clear Biblical principles? Reading this book will certainly stretch and expand your understanding and challenge you to take these principles onto your political 'battlefield' and personal life as well.

Bobbie Patray
President, Tennessee Eagle Forum

It's important for Christians to think clearly about politics. In a day when many Christians dismiss it as "unspiritual" and a pursuit of "worldly power" on one hand, while others are captive to the illusion that politics is the solution for all that ails us, this book by my friend David Fowler is a breath of fresh air. It's thoughtful, articulate, and accessible, and it's worth the investment to read.

John Stonestreet
Speaker and Fellow,
Colson Center for Christian Worldview

Table of Contents

—ɷ—

Preface

—∿∿—

At a time in the life of America and the American church in which many would say the church is too involved in politics and needs to pay less attention to politics, it would seem that a book on "Christian politics" is untimely, unneeded and unwanted. But I disagree.

In this regard, in recent years I have been challenged by something Martin Luther said. Luther, the man whose Ninety-five Theses launched the Protestant Reformation, made the following statement about that place in culture where the church needs to take a strong stand in the face of an overwhelming temptation to retreat:

> If I profess with the loudest voice and clearest exposition every part of the Word of God except that point where the world and the devil are then attacking, I am not professing Christ, no matter how loudly I'm professing Christ. Where the battle rages, there the loyalty of the soldier is proved, and to be steady on all the battlefield besides, is but mere flight and disgrace if he flinches at that point.

If Luther was right, and I believe he was, then perhaps the church would do well to consider where the battle of its day is raging most fiercely and take a stand there.

There is no doubt that today the battle rages in the political realm. It rages in our culture over the issue of whose values and worldview will carry America into the future. Just as importantly, the battle rages in the church—not just over how to engage, but whether to engage at all. It seems that some may even wonder whether in the current political climate a Christian can be engaged in politics and love God and his neighbor well.

If the church is to engage and not flinch where the battle rages today, then it must be engaged in politics. But that is not to say that the church must simply redouble whatever efforts it is making. Evangelist Charles Finney got it right when he said, "The Church must take right ground to politics."

Based on 20 years in politics, I believe what Christianity needs is a basis for engagement in politics, grounded in the Word of God, that puts God front and center and makes Him the object of our engagement. In that regard, I hope to make the case that Christians are not to engage in politics for the mere sake of engagement, for the sake of good citizenship or civic duty, or even for the sake of "saving America." When we do, those things, not God, become the object of our political engagement. They can become idols.

And I certainly hope to disabuse any notion that we Christians are to engage in politics for the sake of laying hold to power. To the contrary, one of the biblical truths we have too often lost sight of is that power belongs not to any man or group of men, but to God. And it is this thought that is central to a right understanding of what I call "the politics of loving God."

Acknowledgments

—ɷ—

This book is the culmination of the love, kindness, encouragement, instruction, and support of a lifetime of wonderful people. To ponder even a moment those who since my earliest days in the church nursery to the present have impacted my life for the good literally brings tears to my eyes. Truly, as the Psalmist said, the "lines have fallen to me in beautiful places."

I hope you all know who you are for I could not name you all without doing an injustice to someone whose name would undoubtedly come to my mind at a later time. Still, I would be remiss not to give special thanks to:

My mom, looking down from heaven, and to my dad. Thank you for the foundation in Christian faith and family that you provided,

My daughter, Allison. Thank you for joy, laughter and, yes, even the tears that let me see more clearly the goodness of my Heavenly Father's heart, and

My wife, Linda. Thank you for being the love of Jesus and grace of God to me for the past 32 years of marriage. "Many daughters have done virtuously, but thou excel them all." My life would have been incomplete without you.

And finally, I give thanks to God for his inexpressible gift of grace in Jesus Christ who loved me in spite of myself. To Him be all the glory both now and forever more.

Introduction

Why Should You Listen to Me?

—ɯ—

The memo was sitting in my chair when I returned to my law office. It was from one of my fellow law partners. It contained his thoughts about a comment I had made to the local newspaper in my capacity as a Tennessee state senator. The newspaper had asked for my thoughts about an attempt to start a club at an area high school for students confused about their sexuality. I had said something to the effect that helping the students would be good so long as the adult supervisor helped them understand the truth about human sexuality and did not affirm or encourage a homosexual lifestyle.

My partner's memo began by making it clear that my statement personally offended him. He then set forth a litany of questions. This is part of what he wrote (emphasis mine):

> Perhaps my next inquiry should be into how you came to the *sure knowledge* that it is a simple question of "right or wrong," rather than a genetic and/or environmentally imposed disposition.

Perhaps you could also *inform* me on what it is that makes a heterosexual person inherently "right" or "better" than a person who is not heterosexual.

Perhaps you have some *new knowledge* about which you can enlighten me on why through all of recorded history there has been a rather constant percentage of gay people? And having helped me with that one, perhaps you can fill me in on your *special knowledge* about how so many of these gay people were outstanding in so many of their human endeavors.

Then, with your *particular abilities of discernment*, you could tell me how so many of your fellow church members are gay (but have not told anyone).

Perhaps you could fill me in, one heterosexual Christian man to another, on what gives you the right or the nerve or even the inclination to be so judgmental and so free with your self-righteous condemnation.[1]

Obviously he did not care much for what I had to say. For having only been officially elected for a little over a week, my time in public office was off to a flying start!

But like my law partner, when it comes to this book, it is only natural that you would wonder if I have "special knowledge" or "new knowledge" concerning the subject of politics and religion. You might ask yourself why you should care about what I have to say. After all, hundreds of people have written on politics and religion, and on politics and Christianity in particular. Some have more formal theological training than I have and some have held higher political office than I have. What makes me unique, a voice to be considered? Well, there are several considerations I would offer.

First, when it comes to the issue of Christian theology, I admit I am not seminary- trained. My understanding of the Scriptures was

learned the hard way, over a lifetime of :
books by theologians, but tempered anc
real life political experiences. Many wh
whose theological backgrounds I admire
never compete, have never grappled witl
regarding politics, government and law i
say that to scorn the value of a seminary de
who studied hard to earn one. And it doesn t mean that I think the
theology of every seminary-trained person who writes on politics is
bad. I just mean that knowing about something and having to try to
"do" what you know are two different things.

Second, when it comes to doing, I served for 12 years in the Tennessee
Senate. I ran against a 26-year incumbent who was chair of the state
Senate's education committee. I have lived out the subject of this
book. Having a microphone stuck in your face for your opinion on
a controversial social issue, knowing that what you say could land
you in trouble with the major media across the nation, makes how
you frame the issue and the theology behind it "come alive" (and,
by the way, I have been in such "trouble" on more than one occasion). Grappling with an issue in the abstract is one thing. Pushing
the button on your legislative desk for or against a law that could
negatively impact millions of lives for a long time if you make the
wrong decision is quite another. I have had to push that button thousands of times.

Third, I have experienced politics from what they sometimes call
"the third house." There is the House and Senate that we learned
about in middle school civics class. But there is another "house"
whose non-elected members are composed of those who lobby
the elected members of the other two "houses." As a lobbyist one
develops yet an even different perspective. As a senator, I held the
power of elected office and people related to me one way. Now, as

I am on the other side of the legislator's desk. So, unlike lobbyists, I know politics from both sides of the desk.

Fourth, I grew up in the church. For some that might be seen as good. Others might think it either bad or irrelevant. In my case, I think it is good, and it is relevant. When I speak to the issues in this book, I come at it from a lifetime of looking at and being part of the church and Christianity.

My perspective on the church is that of an "insider." Growing up, my father was a bi-vocational minister of music, and my parents led the revival music in more churches than I can count. I have served as a minister of music in two different churches in two different areas of the country, served as an elected church officer, taught Sunday school, and belonged to multiple denominations as an adult. So I have not only had the opportunity to observe a diversity of churches and Christians, but to do so from the inside.

Fifth, I have been trained in the study of the law. Having studied law, practiced it, and made it doesn't make me too unique in the world of politics. A number of politicians are lawyers by training and many have practiced law, but it does differentiate my experience and education from that of most seminarians and many lobbyists. There is great value in having studied law both as it is currently taught in law schools and as it is discussed in Scripture.

> **...if what I have to say does not line up with the truth about God as revealed in his Word, then it is rubbish.**

In other words, when it comes to talking about law, government and politics, I could commend to you my rather unique combination of education and experience. However, in listing my "qualifications," I am reminded of what the apostle Paul said: all the things about which he could boast were but rubbish compared to knowing Christ.[3] Likewise, notwithstanding any qualifications I might have, if what I have to say does not line up with the truth about God as revealed in his Word, then it is rubbish. And if that's the case, then my words are just one more "high and lofty thing" being lifted "against the knowledge of God," and should be "cast down.[4]

But if my words are true to who he is, then I hope that, by writing, I will add something useful to the discussion taking place where the battle rages.

Let's begin.

Chapter 1

The Politics of Hate

—⁓—

After almost two decades in politics and speaking to countless Christians about getting involved in politics, I have heard any number of reasons for why they are reluctant to get involved. The one I hear most frequently revolves around not wanting to come across as hateful, thereby turning people off to the gospel. Today Christians are having to decide whether they can be involved in politics and not be hateful.

The decision is really nothing more than deciding how to handle in a godly way the age-old tension for Christians between truth and grace. Grace without the existence of truth is meaningless. Who needs grace if there is no truth our words, actions and attitudes can violate? But truth without grace is often just plain mean, or as some might say today, "hateful." Expressed another way, the tension is between loving our neighbor,

...the tension is between loving our neighbor, which can imply some level of accepting the fact they are *not keeping* God's commandments, and our own calling to love God *by keeping* his commandments.

which can imply some level of accepting the fact they are *not keeping* God's commandments, and our own calling to love God *by keeping* his commandments. This tension is very real in innumerable circumstances, but perhaps there is no place in which the tension is greater, and the effect more significant in terms of the number of people potentially impacted, than in the realm of politics, government and law. Those areas of life can and often do touch all of us. The following story demonstrates the problem.

On June 16, 2012, while on the syndicated radio talk show, *The Ken Coleman Show*, Chick-fil-A president and chief operating officer Dan Cathy said:

> I think we are inviting God's judgment on our nation when we shake our fist at Him and say, "We know better than you as to what constitutes a marriage." I pray God's mercy on our generation that has such a prideful, arrogant attitude to think that we have the audacity to define what marriage is about.[5]

The next month, on July 2, *Biblical Recorder* published an interview with Mr. Cathy. In response to a question about the opposition of some to his company's "support of the traditional family," he replied: "Well, guilty as charged."[6] Mr. Cathy went on to say:

> "We are very much supportive of the family—the biblical definition of the family unit. We are a family-owned business, a family-led business, and we are married to our first wives. We give God thanks for that....We want to do anything we possibly can to strengthen families. We are very much committed to that."[7]

A few weeks later, Floyd Lee Corkins, II, an active volunteer at a community center supporting and providing services to the lesbian, gay, bisexual and transgender (LGBT) community in Washington,

D.C., entered the Washington office of the Family Research Council (FRC) with a gun, 50 rounds of ammunition, and 15 Chick-fil-A sandwiches in his bag. When he brandished his gun, a building supervisor wrestled him to the ground and was shot in the process. As he pulled out his gun, the man said he didn't like FRC's politics.[8] And the reason was that FRC had been labeled a "hate group" for its views on homosexuality by the Southern Poverty Law Center (SPLC).

With these two stories, it was "game on" in the "politics of hate." And it is the "politics of hate" that makes loving God and loving our neighbor so hard in the political realm these days. Put that phrase in any Internet search engine and you'll get page after page of links to articles and videos. But what really is the "politics of hate?"

Dan Cathy was a purveyor of the "politics of hate" because those who support a redefinition of marriage saw his remarks as "hateful." In fact, some politicians thought his comments so "hateful" they even said they didn't want a company with those values located in their community.[9] Students at universities began petitions to have the restaurant removed from their campuses.

After the shooting at FRC, the organization's president held a press conference during which he called on the SPLC to stop fostering an atmosphere of hate by labeling as "hate groups" those groups with which it disagreed. SPLC countered that the charge was "outrageous," saying it didn't label FRC a hate group because of *what* it believed but for the misinformation it spread about homosexuals.[10] The offer by FRC's president to debate the SPLC about the veracity of the information it was condemning went unanswered.[11]

Personally, I am well acquainted with the "politics of hate." As an elected official for 12 years and the head of a pro-family public policy organization for the last eight years, I have had my share of people tell me I'm a "hater" and I'm "hateful." It comes with the territory these days.

But the question that no one seems to be asking, and no one seems to be answering, is "What is hate?" You may be thinking, *everybody knows what hate is*. And we do, at least when it comes to things like the toppings we hate on our pizza. But what does it mean in this context, in the political context? If we can't define what it means in this instance, then we Christians will never be able to answer the question posed at the beginning of this chapter.

In politics it seems like everybody accuses everybody else of engaging in the politics of hate. But surely we aren't all talking about the same thing because that would mean we are all haters. So we just keep talking past one another, and we will continue to do so until we define what it means to hate.

To define "hate" and the "politics of hate," it is best to put them in the context of a specific political issue. For the sake of discussion, we will stick with the issue with which we began this chapter: the definition of marriage. I admit that I oppose same-sex marriage; however, if you think my use of marriage for this discussion makes me a hateful homophobe, then you just proved my point. Today it seems that disagreeing with or opposing the legalization of same-sex marriage makes one hateful *per se*. But why would that be so? I can think of two reasons.

The first justifiable reason for hating something or someone is because that something or someone is unjust, wicked or evil. There has been a violation of that which is just, righteous or good. In that case, an argument could be made that hate is not such a bad thing; it is not wrong to hate injustice or evil. In fact, we find that idea in Scripture and even attributed to God. Today, in Christian circles, we make it sound a little nicer by calling it something like righteous indignation.

So, going back to the specific issue of the legalization of same-sex marriage, disagreeing could be hateful if, in fact, denying marital recognition to two people of the same sex is unjust, wicked or evil. That issue is discussed more fully in footnote 65.

A second reason that disagreeing could be hateful is a belief that, in this world in which tolerance seems to be the cardinal virtue, disagreement itself is hateful. But this creates a conundrum. Each of us, and every organization with differing opinions, would be hateful. If I am hateful because I disagree with you, then by that same logic you are hateful if you disagree with me.

So if disagreement itself is hateful, then being hateful ceases to mean very much. Anyone with a position on anything could be called a "hater" or a "hate group." So mere disagreement can't explain the "politics of hate." I don't think that is what lies behind the phrase as it is used today.

Since this second reason for hating someone or some organization is specious, then labeling someone "hateful," a "hater" or "intolerant" is only meaningful if there is some true, real value at stake that the person so labeled is violating. And the person violating that value can only be morally culpable if they know or should know of the truthfulness of that value. But my sense is that is not what is behind the use of the term today either.

For example, if the purpose of the label was to identify real values and those who are violating them, it would seem that groups like SPLC would be quick to debate FRC about its alleged campaign of misinformation. You would think that those who know the "truth" would be eager to educate those who are misinformed.

But SPLC's response to the debate challenge demonstrates that the purpose of accusing others of engaging in the politics of hate is something else. And it is exactly the opposite of what you'd expect. The purpose is *to avoid debate on the substance of an issue.*

The "politics of hate" is just the modern-day version of the old ad hominem argument.

The "politics of hate" is just the modern-day version of the old *ad hominem* argument. In academic circles that type of argument is known as a logical fallacy — it proves nothing because it tries to discredit the message by discrediting the messenger. In street language it is the equivalent of what we mean when we say, "Hey, don't shoot the messenger!" We all know that the messenger and the message have to be kept separate. *Ad hominem* arguments are meaningless and unconvincing to any reasonable, thinking person.

But here is how the *ad hominem* argument works when it comes to the "politics of hate." We know that a person who does injustice and evil is deserving of the title "hateful." So those who accuse a person of the "politics of hate" hope that by the use of the label they can convince us that the person is, indeed, hateful. And if they can convince us to accept that label, then they know we have accepted the *assumption underlying the accusation*, namely, that the "hateful person" must be doing something unjust or evil.

The "politics of hate" is the lazy man's way of trying to convince us that the person so labeled has done something evil or unjust. In a society in which emotion and feelings are eclipsing in importance critical thinking and reflection, it is easy to get someone to accept the *presumption* behind the label by simply appealing to their emotions and feelings. It is far easier than having to prove that something evil actually occurred. That we accept such arguments today doesn't speak too well for our intelligence and reasoning abilities.

Here is how it played out for me personally in the week between the Chick-fil-A uproar and the FRC shooting. I was on a local television show with other panelists discussing the Chick-fil-A situation[12] and one of the panelists started talking about hate in connection with those who disagree with "marriage equality." I could not let the "hate" comment pass.

My response was that I was tired of debate that used pejorative terms in order to distract from the real issue: namely, what is the nature and purpose of marriage and what kinds of human relationships are consistent with that. You see, *that* issue is one the accusers of hate don't want to really talk about so they distract the audience from the *real* issue. They try to silence all opposition to their view by calling their opponents "hateful."

And why might that work? It is because no one likes to be thought of as hateful. No one wants to become a social outcast. And the accuser also knows that few people like to come to the defense of someone whom others think hateful. That makes them hateful and an outcast too. So many back off and say nothing, and those with nothing substantive to say "win" by default.

> The "politics of hate" is the lazy man's way of trying to convince us that the person so labeled has done something evil or unjust.

It is ingenious politics and very effective. It also happens to be wrong and destructive to the good of a society and a governmental structure that depends on the free flow of ideas and public debate.

Whatever the issue, this tactic works. Convince enough people that a person is hateful, and that it is hateful to agree with that person, then the person so accused and the person's possible supporters will likely shut up.

But for us Christians, as long as we are speaking the truth and doing so graciously, then we need to grapple with something Jesus said about being hated. It is what makes the politics of hate relevant to the politics of loving God.

Chapter 2

Maybe Hate Isn't So Bad After All

—ɷ—

If you're like me, don't you just "hate" some of the things Jesus said? I know that sounds strong, and actually I don't hate them, but some of what he said does make me very uncomfortable. For instance:

> Blessed are you when men hate you and ostracize you, and cast insults at you and spurn your name as evil, for the sake of the Son of Man. Be glad in that day, and leap for joy, for behold, your reward is great in heaven; for in the same way their fathers used to treat the prophets. Luke 6:22-23 (NASB)

What? Am I supposed to *like* being hated? What in the world was Jesus saying? And what in the world does it have to do with the politics of loving God? That is, after all, the reason you probably picked up the book.

To make sense of this statement and to make sense of everything else in this book, you need to know that my beliefs are grounded in this one simple statement with which the Bible starts: "In the beginning,

God created the heavens and the earth." The New Testament parallel appears at the start of the Gospel of John:

> In the beginning was the Word, and the Word was with God, and the Word was God. He was in the beginning with God. All things were made through Him, and without Him nothing was made that was made. In Him was life … .[13]

Actually, even this belief presupposes another belief that I might as well get out of the way. It is increasingly controversial, even in the church. So, I will just go on and say it: I believe that the Bible is the Word of God. Even among many who call themselves Christians, that is an increasingly "extreme" position, and among those who are not Christians, it is perhaps incomprehensible. Many might say it is stupid, unscientific,[14] or irrational, but thankfully, however, our current culture does not seem quite ready to say such a belief is itself hateful, though some probably would.[15]

That being said, here is what I mean by "I believe the Bible is the Word of God." I like what I heard some minister once say in response to whether he took all the words of the Bible literally, "I take them all seriously." I would hope that at a minimum all professing Christians would take the words in the Bible seriously. After all, even some who don't take it to be God's Word have found in it valuable principles by which to live.[16]

Perhaps what I mean by taking the Bible seriously can best be summed up by what Dr. Del Tackett, developer of The Truth Project®, calls "a haunting question." Toward the very end of his first lecture on the existence and source of truth, he asks what reality is, and he makes the point that we call crazy those who do not perceive reality correctly. Then he asked if we thought the Bible revealed to us reality as it really was. He picked up his Bible and asked the haunting question: "Do you believe that what you believe is really real?"

He continued with a couple of thoughts that I collectively paraphrase like this: "If I really believed this (holding up his Bible). If I really believed the stories in this book, I wouldn't have trouble praying. If I really believed that God was saying to me, 'Hey, Del, pull up a chair; let's talk,' I wouldn't have trouble praying. I'd have trouble leaving! Do you really believe what you believe is really real?"

For sure that question has haunted me. Practically every day and in multiple situations, I find myself asking what it is in that moment I believe and whether it is the truth or a lie. It is an important question because what we believe determines what we do.

> ...I find myself asking what it is in that moment I believe and whether it is the truth or a lie.

I remember as part of a church Sunday school project raking the leaves at the home of an elderly woman. After the small group of us had worked for a while, the woman asked if we wanted to come in for something to drink. We did and found her boiling the water she eventually served us. She told us that "they" were poisoning her water so she had to boil the poison out before she could let us have a drink. As crazy as that was, what would you and I have been doing if we believed what she believed? We would have been boiling our drinking water too!

So when Jesus said that, as Christians, we are blessed if men revile us and say all manner of evil about us—like calling us "haters"—did he mean it? If so, what are we to make of it? Could it be that being hated maybe isn't all that bad? If we are going to take the words in the Bible seriously, then the answer must be, "Yes, he meant what he said." But did he mean Christians needed to like being hated? I don't think so.

Jesus knew that if we followed him we would be hated. He even said that if people hated him—and some hated him enough that they killed him—then we should expect to be hated too. I believe Jesus meant these words to be an encouragement to us when the inevitable accusation of "hater" came. To look at it another way, if we Christians remain silent because we don't want to be accused of being hateful, then we need to ask ourselves this question: "Were these words of Jesus meant to be an encouragement to us to stand firm in the face of opposition, ridicule and scorn, or was Jesus just wrong on this one?" *That* is a haunting question! It is one I ask myself regularly.

> **We are going to have to understand that *being* hateful is different from someone *thinking* we are hateful or *calling* us hateful.**

If you and I are going to love God well (and loving God well entails loving our neighbor well), then we are going to have to get used to being called a hater. Jesus said things that evoked hatred toward him, but he was not hateful for telling them the truth. We are going to have to understand that *being* hateful is different from someone *thinking* we are hateful or *calling* us hateful. We will never answer the question whether Christians can be involved in politics and not be hateful if we allow the judgment of other people and their perception of us[17] to define that term for us rather than God as revealed to us in the ways of Jesus.

The politics of hate really puts at issue how much we really want to "be" like Jesus, which we Christians say we want to be. In this regard, I have come to understand that if Jesus himself "learned obedience" to the Father "by the things which he suffered,"[18] then I had better not be deterred by the possibility of suffering for what I believe. If suffering is a deterrent, then I need to stop saying I want to be like Jesus. From what I have seen in myself and in more than a few Christians that I have met along the way, it looks like the "politics of loving God" is going to have to overcome more than the "politics of hate": *it is going to have to overcome our fear.*

Chapter 3

Power Politics

—ɯ—

E ver heard the expression, "The power of the ballot box"? I bet you have. The expression is an acknowledgment, usually without much reflection, that voting is the exercise of power. But when we do take a minute to think about it, we realize that, in voting, we are transferring the power we hold as citizens to the person we elect to hold office in our civil government.

Civil government involves power. That is not too revelatory. Politics, as distinguished from actual governing, is the channel through which the power of civil government is transferred from one person to another and the medium in which we debate the purposes for which the power of government should be used.

But before we go too far with these two thoughts, we need to go back to the fundamental premise of this book (and of the Bible); namely, in the beginning, God. If you and I, as Christians, are going to take that assertion seriously, then whatever else we might want to say about how God created the heavens and the earth and how long it took him to do it, then we have to believe that whatever reality there is comes from God, in the final analysis. It has to. He is the ultimate beginning. And if we prefer to work our way backward from a present reality to its origin then he is the final stop on the logic train.

From a biblical worldview, power belongs to, and comes from, God.[19] Not only does Scripture say this explicitly, but it could not be otherwise if God is truly in the beginning and everything else flows from Him. Where else could power come from?

...in the final analysis all power ultimately comes from God, even the power of civil government.

But it isn't just "spiritual" power that comes from God; in the final analysis all power ultimately comes from God, even the power of civil government. Colossians 1:16 states that part of what God created was "thrones," "rulers" and "authorities." Thus, it is not surprising that Jesus would tell Pilate—a government official no less—that he "would have no authority over [him] unless it had been given [him] from above."[20]

The Bible is pretty clear here, and Romans 13:1-4 is the classic biblical summation of the relationship between the power and authority of God and that of civil government. Verse one reads:

> Let every soul be subject to the governing authorities. For there is no authority except from God, and the authorities that exist are appointed by God.

The authority held by a government official finds its origin in God.[21] Period. Romans 13 simply builds upon the premise that power belongs to God.

Those who would disregard Scripture realize that power has to come from somewhere. Men like John Locke and Jean-Jacques Rousseau come to mind. They recognized that the power of civil government could not come from the government itself. That would have been circular reasoning. So what are some popular alternatives?

Some, and perhaps most, might say that the power of civil government is derived from the power we as human beings hold as individuals over ourselves.[22] But as we will discuss in Chapter 8, that thought is fraught with problems.

Those who accept naturalism or materialism as their worldview, a view that is grounded in some aspect of the material world (e.g. matter or energy) as ultimate reality, say it is somewhere found in the "state of nature." But they are stuck having to explain how the kind of power we are talking about, which is immaterial, came into being in a purely material universe.

Those who might argue that the power of civil government comes from our constitution forget that not all countries have a constitution. Furthermore, if civil government's power comes from a constitution, then every constitution I have ever read has sown within itself the seeds for destroying that power. By amendment, we can essentially abolish the constitution we have and start over. So, if we believe civil government's power comes from the constitution, then where does it go when a constitution is abolished and where does it come from when the new constitution is adopted? A constitution merely orders how the power of civil government can be exercised and by whom. It is not the source of power.

> ...if one accepts the possibility of a Creator, it is not hard to accept the biblical assertion that the power of civil government comes from God.

Thus, if one accepts the possibility of a Creator, it is not hard to accept the biblical assertion that the power of civil government comes from God. If that is the case, however, then citizens who are eligible voters under our form of government, who hold the "power of the ballot box," need to understand that their power comes from God. The same is true for the government official. In our form of civil government, the power of God is mediated through the people to the government official. The government official is thus doubly accountable—to God and to the people through whom God allowed his power to be delegated. This is a pretty weighty thought for all of us, but one that is often given very little consideration.

If you are reading this and you are a government official or hope to be one some day, let me give you some good news that flows from this thought. For those of you who are not in that category, read on with an eye toward how well those you have voted for might understand and appreciate what is said. John Calvin, one of the great sixteenth century leaders of the Protestant Reformation, said it very well:

> [N]o man can doubt that civil authority is, in the sight of God, not only sacred and lawful, but the most sacred, and by far the most honourable, of all stations in mortal life....This consideration ought to be constantly present to the minds of magistrates, since it is fitted to...afford singular consolation, smoothing the difficulties of their office, which are certainly numerous and weighty.

In other words, as a government official, you are not doing some "dirty," "profane," "secular" work. You are therefore not just administering some "necessary evil."

As a former elected office holder, I have heard all of these adjectives used to describe civil government, and, unfortunately, I have heard them from Christians. For those Christians who have said things like that, then John Calvin has a word for them also:

> In regard to those who are not debarred by all these passages of Scripture from presuming to inveigh against this sacred ministry [of the government official], as if it were a thing abhorrent from religion and Christian piety, what else do

they do than assail God himself, who cannot but be insulted when his servants are disgraced?

Now for the government official, here is the sobering news that flows from the fact that the power you hold comes from God. Again John Calvin said:

> How will they [the magistrates] dare to admit iniquity to their tribunal, when they are told that it is the throne of the living God? How will they venture to pronounce an unjust sentence with that mouth which they understand to be an ordained organ of divine truth? With what conscience will they subscribe impious decrees with that hand which they know has been appointed to write the acts of God? In a word, if they remember that they are the vicegerents of God, it behooves them to watch with all care, diligence, and industry, that they may in themselves exhibit a kind of image of the Divine Providence, guardianship, goodness, benevolence, and justice. And let them constantly keep the additional thought in view, that if a curse is pronounced on him that "doeth the work of the Lord deceitfully," a much heavier curse must lie on him who deals deceitfully in a righteous calling....This admonition ought justly to have the greatest effect upon them; for *if they sin in any respect, not only is injury done to the men whom they wickedly torment, but they also insult God himself, whose sacred tribunals they pollute.* (emphasis added)

Those are strong words. And they are sobering words for the Christian in a position of authority in government, particularly judges and policy makers. Do the people have a better picture, or "image" in the words of Calvin, of who God is because of the judgments reflected by the votes and decisions our elected officials make and because of the way in which they comport themselves in the execution of their duties?

Perhaps the clearest picture of this, the one that frequently came to my mind as an elected official, is that of Nebuchadnezzar. Though Nebuchadnezzar was not elected, like our elected officials, as king, he did hold authority in the realm of civil government. One day, while walking in the palace, he said:

> Is not this great Babylon, that I have built for a royal dwelling by my mighty power and for the honor of my majesty?[23]

God's reaction was immediate. Scripture records that *"while the word [was] in the king's mouth,* a voice fell from heaven, [saying], 'O king Nebuchadnezzar, to you it is spoken; The kingdom has departed from you.'" The great king was consigned to wander in the fields like an ox for a period of time.

Nebuchadnezzar committed two errors. The first was that he forgot where his power came from, and the second was that he didn't understand the purpose for which he held that power. His power came from God and the purpose for which he held it was to glorify God, not himself or his kingdom.[24] God will not give his glory to another.[25]

I sometimes think of it as God saying to Nebuchadnezzar that if what he said was what he really thought, then he was as dumb as an ox and everyone was going to know it because he would begin living like one. Interestingly, when the appointed time had run, we find that Nebuchadnezzar's "understanding returned" to him when he "lifted [his] eyes to heaven." It was when he looked up to heaven that he knew what was really real, and he said:

> My understanding returned unto me; and I blessed the most High, and I praised and honoured Him who lives forever For His dominion [is] an everlasting dominion, and His kingdom

[is] from generation to generation. And all the inhabitants of the earth [are] reputed as nothing; He does according to His will in the army of heaven, and [among] the inhabitants of the earth. No one can restrain His hand, or say to him, "What have you done?"[26]

Before we leave this Chapter, we must recognize in the story of Nebuchadnezzar a sobering thought for the Christian citizen. If political or governmental power comes from God and is to be used for the glory of God, then that means the citizen's vote (and the government official's loyalty) do not belong to a political party, a union, or a trade or professional association. It does not belong to anything that can be referred to by any of the acronyms so prevalent in politics today. It belongs to God, and that also means that we are not free to use the power we hold however we might wish.

Chapter 4

Loving God

—∿—

It was the morning of February 29, 1996. I was serving as a Tennessee state senator. As the Senate convened, small shafts of light eked between the folds of the heavy curtains that cloaked the windows of the Senate chamber. The television camera lights created a brightness normally missing within the smoke-encrusted walls of the chamber. The cameras were rolling. Reporters were hanging on every word and typing away in their booths at the side of the chamber.

To me it had the feel of one of those professional wrestling grudge matches you see on television. Picture it with the liberals in mainstream media serving as the announcer, describing to their audience what was about to unfold: "Ladies and gentlemen! In this corner, weighing in with a large brain filled with knowledge is the progressive liberal, and his opponent, in the opposite corner, weighing in with a pea-sized brain is the social conservative."

At issue was whether Tennessee would adopt a Defense of Marriage Act, a law defining marriage as between one man and one woman and making the recognition of any other form of marriage void as against the state's public policy. I knew that if I rose to speak in favor of the act, that just one slip of a sentence in debate, failing to fend off one question well, and the press would put me down for the count.

And as I expected, the Senate's most liberal intellectual rose to ask questions, and the act's prime sponsor yielded the floor to me for the answers. The senator asked me all kinds of questions, but his last one and my answer to it ended the questioning. He asked me:

> Do you not agree it would be a societal improvement if the people of this state encouraged people who are at high risk of getting AIDs to stay committed to each other [by allowing them to marry]. Would that not serve society well?

My response was:

> Perhaps it would, but there is nothing that prevents them from being committed in that relationship today. They can be as committed as they want to be.[27]

...I was shocked by her comment because she had never agreed with my politics.... Actually my point didn't "suck" if my argument was logical.

As I passed by the media room after the session was over, a reporter said that she really did appreciate my arguments and enjoyed listening to me debate because my arguments were so logical and in order from point to point.

To be honest, I was shocked by her comment because she had never agreed with my politics. So I asked her why she didn't agree with me if my arguments were logical. Her response: "Because your point sucks." Actually my point didn't "suck" if my argument was logical. Whether she knew it or not, what she really disagreed with—what really sucked to her—was not my point, but my premise, the foundational principles upon which I had built the logic of my argument.

The premise of any argument is foundational. But it is also important that critical terms used in the argument are not ambiguous or capable of multiple meanings. If they are, then your words and argument will be twisted and the meaning of your point will be undermined or lost.

But here is the flip side of the coin: if we accept the premises of the arguments and the way the key terms are defined and there is no flaw in the logic that follows, then if we don't like the conclusion we only have two alternatives:

I guess a third alternative is to live like the truth is a lie.

change our opinion and accept the new conclusion as the truth or re-examine our definitions and premises. I guess a third alternative is to live like the truth is a lie.

Anyway, the logic of my argument in this book — that there is relationship between loving God and my fellow man, on the one hand, and engaging in politics on the other — rests upon two things: the two premises laid out in the preceding chapters; namely, that God is in the beginning, and that the truth of that premise should be taken seriously.[28]

But before my analysis of the relationship between politics and loving God will make any sense, we have to define the nature of our relationship to God. If the two premises I have laid out are accepted, then our initial point of reference for defining that relationship would be found in the creation story told in the first two chapters of Genesis. From those chapters, we would conclude that we are created beings and, as such, we are dependent on our Creator for our existence and contingent upon his provision. I am not in any real sense of the term, "my own." The second reference point is that because everything comes from God, in the final analysis, everything is really his. It is on the foundation of these two points that we can conclude that whatever comes into our possession or control, having come from or through God, our relationship to it is that of a steward. Or to put it in less theological terms, we are trustees of whatever it is we possess.

A stewardship or trustee relationship implies certain things. Because whatever I possess is not really mine, I am not free to use it for my personal benefit to the detriment of the owner. I can only use it for the benefit of the true owner according to the owner's instructions.

These limits applicable to a trustee don't just apply to those who seek to live according to "God's Law." The laws of civil government reflect the same principle.[29] We could say it is just common sense. Something we all really know. Ever had anybody borrow something from you and do with it something you didn't approve? If so, you get my point. We don't like or appreciate our things being misused, particularly if it comes back to us broken.

Now, in the church, we seem to get this thought theologically — that what we have comes from God and we are accountable to him for what we do with it — when it comes to our time, our talent and our treasure. If you have attended a church for any sustained period of time, you have heard the sermons about stewardship that seem to come around church budget time. We understand the concept of stewardship. Whether we really believe it to the point we act like it is another question.

But let's put this thought about stewardship on hold for a moment and ask ourselves the question, "What does it mean to love God?" Thankfully, we don't have to guess. Jesus tells us repeatedly that if we love him, one of the things we will do is keep his commandments.[30] In other words, Jesus is saying that we can say we love him all we want, but the proof is in the proverbial pudding of what we do, not what we say.

So if God gives us "stuff" to be stewards over and if we show our love for him by keeping his commandments, then stewarding well what we have been given would have to be a way of showing our love for him. And stewarding something well means using it for the benefit of the real owner, in this case God, and according to the real owner's instructions. It is here where the "politics" of loving God takes root.

Yet, "politics" has become a dirty word in the church. The church doesn't like to talk about political things. Most often, at best, a church will encourage its members to register to vote and maybe even remind them to vote. Even then, though, the announced motivation is usually couched in terms of good citizenship or civic duty. However, for the Christian it is so much more than that. It is an act of stewardship!

If voting is an exercise of power and if that power, in the final analysis, belongs to God, then voting should be seen as an act of stewardship toward God, of loving God well. But voting is only a first step in the act of stewardship. The second step is to evaluate the issues and the candidates according to God's "platform," the precepts and the principles found in his Word. When we do these things, we are engaging in politics for the sake of stewarding well the authority God has entrusted to us in the civil realm. Faithful stewardship *is* an expression of our love for God. And loving God is not hateful.

> **If voting is an exercise of power and if that power, in the final analysis, belongs to God, then voting should be seen as an act of stewardship toward God, of loving God well.**

This is really nothing more than a particular application of what Paul meant when he said, "it is no longer I who lives, but Christ lives in me."[31] The way Christians "do" politics should be

Christians *can* engage in politics without being hateful *if* our purpose and focus are defined in terms of God!

understandable only in relationship to who God, in Christ, is and who we are in relation to him. If it is any other way, then we are not allowing Christ to define who we are and what we do. Therefore, in answer to our original question, Christians *can* engage in politics without being hateful *if* our purpose and focus are defined in terms of God!

If that is so, then why would our ministers, elders and deacons not want the Christians placed by God under their charge to understand the issues? Why would they not want them to know where the candidates stand on those issues? Perhaps, more importantly, why do so many of us who sit in the pews object so strenuously if they do? Not to educate and equip Christians in this area of life is like telling people they need to be good stewards of their money and then never offering them any teaching on the subject or even a mid-week course from an organization like Crown Ministries©. How are they going to know how to be good stewards of their money or of their political power if they are not taught, if they are not equipped?

Sadly, the prevailing view within the church is that teaching on subjects that intersect with issues (and maybe even specific policies) being debated in the political realm is off limits. In doing this we have divorced God from the very power with which he imbued civil government (and in our form of government, that he entrusted to voters) and that, as "owner" of that power, is subject to him. It shows that we have failed to see politics as an expression of a love of God that is expressed in stewarding well the power he has entrusted to us. Not to engage in politics from even a minimum level of stewardship is not only not loving God but, paraphrasing Calvin's words, are we not insulting God by such thinking (see page 34-35)?

Chapter 5

Getting Off Track

—ɯ—

If what I have said so far about the source of power is true and if Christians actually love God well when they faithfully steward the power entrusted to them by him, then a natural question is, "How did we get so far off track?" That is a good question. And getting "off track" is a good way to think about it.

I had a friend who loved trains. He had the most impressive miniature train set I have ever seen in anyone's home. Unlike my simple train set that just went in a circle, he had the ability to switch a train to a different set of tracks. And that is a pretty good picture of what has happened in America politically. Over time we allowed our nation and our political system to get switched from the biblical worldview tracks upon which our journey began to a set of tracks grounded in a humanistic, secular worldview.

Those who want to deny that the tracks that guided our nation's journey at the beginning were grounded in a biblical worldview probably don't know what a biblical worldview is or, if they do, then they haven't read our Declaration of Independence.

While this is not the place to flesh out all that a biblical worldview incorporates, suffice it to say that it typically encompasses three main categories: creation, fall and redemption.[32] Every worldview touches on at least the first three aspects of this framework. Every worldview has some explanation for the origin of things, what we could call Ultimate Reality.[33] In Christian theology this is the doctrine of creation. Every worldview also has an explanation for what's wrong with the world. In Christian theology this is the doctrine of the Fall, the sin of Adam and Eve. And every worldview proposes some solution to the problem, the means of redemption. In Christian theology the solution is the death and resurrection of Jesus Christ.

Looking then at the Declaration of Independence, we see that the foundational belief in the document was a belief in a Creator. We asserted our right to independence from England on the basis of the "laws of Nature and Nature's God." And we asserted that one of the laws of nature that had been violated was the denial of those rights "endowed" to us "by our Creator."

In addition, the very structure of our federal government was built on a keen understanding of the concept of the fallenness of man. In Federalist Paper 51, James Madison summed it up this way:

> It may be a reflection on human nature, that such devices [as checks and balances] should be necessary to control the abuses of government. *But what is government itself, but the greatest of all reflections on human nature?* If men were angels, no government would be necessary. If angels were to govern men, neither external nor internal controls on government would be necessary. (emphasis added)

That is why I say our nation's beginning rested on the foundation of a biblical worldview: the existence of the Creator and the fallenness of man.

While our nation has not always governed in a manner consistent with its foundational views, it was after the publication of Charles Darwin's *Origin of the Species* in 1859 that our foundational worldview began to come under serious attack. The worldview reflected in Darwin's book, that the natural world could be explained without reference to a Creator, went on trial in 1925. It was the infamous Scopes trial.

...our nation's beginning rested on the foundation of a biblical worldview: the existence of the Creator and the fallenness of man.

The legal outcome of the trial proved irrelevant compared to the cultural fallout. Darwin's worldview advanced and Christians, increasingly ridiculed and uncertain of how to respond, retreated. Generally speaking the church allowed the Creator to be relegated to a supernatural realm where we Christians could "touch" him through spiritual exercises like prayer, Bible reading and church attendance. By putting God in a proverbial box up on a shelf in our "spiritual closet," it made things easier for the Christian to live in the "living room" of what we call everyday life here on earth. It allowed us to avoid having to answer questions about him relative to the natural realm.

But retreat or its cultural equivalent—trying to maintain the status quo—never advances the kingdom of God. Over time, the chasm grew larger between the supernatural, where God had been relegated, and the natural world in which we spent all our time working and relating to other people. As a result, the influence of Darwin's philosophy on the "things of this world" grew. God became less and less relevant to our everyday lives here in the natural realm. The American train of thought switched tracks, and as a result, America as a nation started traveling down a different set of tracks. This has many dimensions; however, for the purpose of this book, all we will consider is its influence on our view of law and civil government.

That the American view of law and government is now running on a different set of tracks from those on which it began was perhaps nowhere more clearly stated than in the United States Supreme Court's 1948 decision in *McCollum v. Board of Education*:[34]

> [T]he First Amendment rests upon the premise that both *religion* and government can best work to achieve their lofty aims if each is *left free from the other in their respective spheres* ...

There you have it: religion (as distinguished from the ecclesiastical institution called "the church") and government have their own spheres and, according to the Court, it is best if they never intersect. God was in the sphere of the supernatural, and law and civil government were in the sphere of the natural. And the two spheres were to be kept distinct from each other. This was a clear statement concerning the compartmentalization of God relative to law and government, and of his irrelevance to the subject.

Which worldview is being reflected among a majority of Christians and our churches' pulpits: God's or Darwin's?

Sadly this is exactly the view of a majority of Christians and ministers in America today when it comes to religion and issues intersecting with politics. It can't help but make one wonder which worldview is being reflected among a majority of Christians and our churches' pulpits: God's or Darwin's.

Anyway, the worldview espoused by the U.S. Supreme Court in 1948 is completely different from the view of the relationship between God and government found, for example, in Article IX, Section II of the Tennessee Constitution that dates back to 1870. That provision, which is not unique to Tennessee, states:

> No person who denies the being of God or a future state of rewards and punishments shall hold any office in the civil department of this state.[35]

In other words, contrary to what the Supreme Court would say 78 years later, those who wrote the Tennessee Constitution said that if your view of God and your responsibilities as an elected official didn't connect at least on Judgment Day, Tennesseans didn't want you holding office.

Today, as a practical matter, we insist on exactly the opposite. We want to make sure our elected officials are willing to and can, in fact, lay aside their religious views when they evaluate policy issues. They may be able to do that, as increasing numbers of them do, but the practical and negative fallout is very real for citizens and for society at large. Moreover, the practical negative fallout on Judgment Day will also be very real.

Chapter 6

Praise and Punishment

—◊◊◊◊—

During my 12 years in the state Senate, I would conservatively estimate that I sat through more than 2,300 meetings with individuals or groups of individuals asking me to support or oppose some kind of legislation. And that was just at my legislative office in Nashville during the four or five months the legislature was in session.

During these meetings I heard all kinds of reasons for voting for or against something. But one thing I never heard was, "Senator, I think this proposed legislation is bad public policy, and it will promote and encourage evil. So I hope you will vote for it." As a matter of sheer "luck" one might think the odds would be in favor of there being at least one such conversation out of more than 2,300. But no, not one.

Of course no one would expect any such conversation. And it is because we all know that the law should promote what is good, certainly not restrain it. Conversely, we all know that the law should restrain or punish what is evil, certainly not try to foster or encourage it. Every person who came to my office knew that truth and acted

> **...we all know that the law should promote what is good, certainly not restrain it.**

accordingly. It was a truth they all knew whether they had thought about it or could have articulated it. Not surprisingly, Scripture confirms what common sense tells us.

As noted previously, the seminal chapter on the subject of civil government's purpose is Romans 13. In that chapter we looked at the first verse to find the source of civil government's authority. With respect to civil government's purpose, we need to look at two other verses:

> 3 For rulers are not a terror to good works, but to evil. Do you want to be unafraid of the authority? Do what is good, and you will have praise from the same. 4 For he is God's minister to you for good. But if you do evil, be afraid; for he does not bear the sword in vain; for he is God's minister, an avenger to [execute] wrath on him who practices evil. Romans 13:3-4

Consistent with my experience as a legislator, the passage speaks of doing good and doing evil. But the passage only speaks of *action* by civil government in the negative. By that I mean it only speaks of the government taking action to restrain or punish an evil. Even the exhortation to "do what is good" is in the context of not having to be in "terror" of what the civil government might do. If civil government is operating biblically, those who do good should have nothing to fear.

Similarly verse 4 says that the civil government "bears the sword," and it is to execute, for God, His wrath on those who "practice" evil. Swinging the proverbial sword at those who are doing evil is certainly an action, and, again, the action is negative in the sense of restraining or punishing evil.

This same thought is found in Galatians 5:22-23. There, after listing the fruit of the spirit, the apostle Paul says that "against such things there is no law."[36] Here the clear implication is that the law would take action "against" things that are not good. And conversely, the law would not punish or restrain that which is good.

By implication then, Galatians affirms our interpretation of the passage in Romans; namely, that the law is a "negative" type action, a negation of or an attack on those things that are not good. The law is a restraining influence, stopping one from doing "bad" things or, alternatively, executing justice if the bad things are done contrary to the law's prohibition. But this passage also helps us see that the law is not *making* a person *do* good things.

If we go back to verses 3 and 4 in Romans 13, we see a similar thought relative to the law and doing good. In those verses it is the citizen doing the good, not the civil government. The civil government's role in that passage is limited to praising those who do good.

Biblically, civil government can recognize what is good and, by praising it, encourage good, but it cannot make people be good, at least not in any sense that God would actually care about. As Scripture says, "By works of the law, no flesh shall be justified in his sight."[37] God's own judgment on the law was that it was powerless to make one good; thus the need for the redeeming and transforming work of Christ and the power of the Holy Spirit.

> **Biblically, civil government can recognize what is good and, by praising it, encourage good, but it cannot make people be good,**

This interpretation of Galatians 5 and Romans 13 is further supported by 1 Peter 2:

13 Therefore submit yourselves to every ordinance of man for the Lord's sake, whether to the king as supreme, 14 or to governors, as to those who are sent by him for the punishment of evildoers and [for the] praise of those who do good.

Here again we see the civil government's two-fold role: on the one hand, it is praising those who are doing good, ostensibly for the purpose of encouraging more good to be done, and on the other hand, it is engaging in the *act* (doing something *to* someone) of punishing.

So, according to Scripture, the law should restrain or punish evil and encourage the good. However, that leaves us with the very interesting question: "How do we determine what is good and what is evil?"

Chapter 7

Who Says?

—✖—

Near the end of my last year in the state Senate, I had a very interesting exchange with a leader for the American Civil Liberties Union (ACLU). The two of us had just concluded a "debate," if that's what you can even call the expression of opposing viewpoints on an early morning talk show. The debate was about a proposed amendment to the state constitution that might restore to the legislature the power to enact certain regulations regarding abortion such as an abortion-specific informed consent law, or a law requiring a period of reflection on that information prior to an abortion. The amendment was necessary because those regulations had been ruled unconstitutional by our state Supreme Court.[38]

During the interview, I kept trying to get the ACLU representative to define what it was that was being aborted. But the advocate for the ACLU just replied by insisting that a woman had a "right to reproductive healthcare." After the show while exchanging parting pleasantries in the studio parking lot, I asked the representative to help me understand where the asserted "right to reproductive healthcare" came from since, in her opinion, the amendment was morally wrong

55

even though the constitutionally mandated amendment process was being followed.

When the representative didn't seem to understand what I was getting at, I explained that the right could not have come from the state constitution, because the constitution could be amended and even abolished. Since we were, in fact, following the process laid out in the constitution for an amendment, I wanted to know where the right came from since, even by following the amendment process, the amendment itself was morally wrong, according to her.

The rub, I said, was who was to decide which of us was right.

When again no clear answer was forthcoming, I explained why I asked; namely, that our rights had to come from somewhere, and because the ACLU rejected the possibility that those rights came from a Creator God, such as our founding fathers believed, then I didn't know where the asserted right came from. I then suggested that if the right didn't come from God, then the only other source was us, humanity. The rub, I said, was who was to decide which of us was right. And in this case, since our constitution said that our difference on this issue would be resolved by majority vote, then if more people agreed with me about abortion then, by definition, the asserted right vanished. Based on a worldview that excluded a Creator God who established a moral order to His universe, then the representative was left with only an argument or a position, but not a right in any real sense of that word.

As our conversation reflected, the nice thing about this question of right and wrong is that it is not that hard; there aren't but two basic answers. This is not like trying to answer your restaurant server who, three minutes after you sit down, asks you what you want off their lengthy menu. To our question the only two answers are God or man. That's it. Take your pick.

In an article published in the *Duke Law Journal* back in 1979, the late Yale law professor, Arthur Leff, looked at both of these answers. His goal was to determine which one would actually work when it came to providing a sense of real authority behind the law. In other words, he was trying to find a basis upon which we could agree that a law *should be* obeyed, because the authority behind the determination that the law was "good" was unquestionable. It is a masterful analysis of this question. He likens it to the rhetorical question asked by the playground bully who, when told by his victim to go away, responds with, "Says who?"

Professor Leff said, "The question really is whether there is any person or set of persons whose generation of law is entitled to final respect." In other words, "Who or what can authoritatively settle among us what is good and what is evil such that, whatever the law is, we *ought* to obey it." (emphasis added)

He began his search for an answer to the question of where such authority could be found with the statement:

> "If the law is 'not a brooding omnipresence in the sky,' then it can be only one place: in us. If we are trying to find a substitute final evaluator [for the God of the Bible], it must be one of us, some of us, all of us, but it cannot be anything else."

In other words, if that authority is not a supernatural God, "[w]ho among us...ought to be able to declare 'law'" that ought to be obeyed?

After rejecting the possibility that the God of the Bible exists and examining all the alternative theories offered over the years, he determined that "there cannot be any normative system ultimately based on anything except human will."[39] He then concluded his article:

> "All I can say is this: it looks as if we are all we have. Given what we know about ourselves and each other, this is an

extraordinarily unappetizing prospect; looking around the world, it appears that if all men are brothers, the ruling model is Cain and Abel. Neither reason, nor love, nor even terror, seems to have worked to make us 'good,' and worse than that, there is no reason why anything should. Only if ethics were something unspeakable by us, could law be unnatural, and therefore unchallengeable. As things now stand, everything is up for grabs....There is in the world such a thing as evil. [All together now:] Sez who? God help us."

There are many in our culture like Professor Leff. They do not want to consider the possibility that there is a God whose nature and character determines good and evil. They also do not want to consider the possibility that God has communicated to us propositionally enough information for us to know what we need to know about what is good and evil. But in my experience, I have found that there are many Christians who, as a practical matter, are no different. They either give no consideration to God and his Word when it comes to law and government, or they only give them lip service. Their hearts and minds are far from him. If both camps are honest, they despair that the alternative is not a good solution either.

This is a good place to remember the story about the reporter who thought my argument for natural marriage was logical but said she hated my point or conclusion. As was said there, if the conclusion we reach based on our premises doesn't work—and Leff's premises left him with something unpalatable, unworkable and inconsistent with his experience regarding good and evil—then we need to reconsider our premises. God loves us too much just to let us ignore him.

Chapter 8

Loving My Neighbor

—⚋—

If one accepts what has been said so far, then the question that remains is what does this look like in the real world? What does it mean for the civil government to encourage good and punish evil? That is a great question, but before we get there we need to understand one other reason why getting the right answer is so important. As was said in Chapter 4, loving God well by stewarding the authority he has entrusted to us should be a very real incentive to be involved in politics. However, there is another incentive: loving our neighbor.

> **What possible connection could there be between politics and loving my neighbor?**

What possible connection could there be between politics and loving my neighbor? One answer is that if there is a connection between our engagement in politics and loving God, then there must be a connection to loving our neighbor. Loving our neighbor is the horizontal expression of our vertical love for God. But there is another way to answer that question, and it depends on how we understand the nature of law.

To understand that, we should ask ourselves the question, "Why is it that the law *must* encourage good and punish evil?" As stated in Chapter 6, Scripture and our own experience tell us that the law must do that. The answer to why this is so is found in the nature of law as revealed by Scripture and experience.

Looking first at Scripture, two passages will suffice in our attempt to understand the nature of law.

> I would not have known sin except through the law. For I would not have known covetousness unless the law had said, "You shall not covet."[40]

> Therefore the law was our tutor [to bring us] to Christ, that we might be justified by faith.[41]

From these passages we see that the law has an educative effect. It informs our ethical judgments about right and wrong. In fact, the latter verse, found in Galatians, says that the law, by its righteous demands and its proscriptions regarding unrighteousness, is used by God to convince and convict us of our own unrighteousness and our need for a savior.

Experience also bears out this interpretation of Scripture. For example, the United States Supreme Court bore witness to the educative affect of the law in its 1992 decision in *Planned Parenthood v. Casey*. In the context of upholding a right to abortion, the Court said:

> [F]or two decades...people have organized their intimate relationships and made choices that *define their views* of themselves and their places in society in reliance on the availability of abortion in the event that contraception should fail....(emphasis added)[42]

In other words, after two decades the laws making abortion available changed the way we view ourselves. The law helped re-educate us. While the Court did not specify the ways in which our views changed, one would have to be blind not to see that over the last 40 years our views have changed regarding the nature and purpose of human sexuality, marriage, the sacredness and value of human life, and the relative importance of child-bearing and parenting vis-a-vis advance-

In other words, after two decades the laws making abortion available changed the way we view ourselves.

ment in career, education and material well-being. Another way in which our views have been changed by the effect of legalized abortion is that today too many people treat children more like a commodity than a gift and blessing from the Lord. Consider the field of assisted reproductive technologies.[43]

While such technologies have been used to help many married couples conceive, the unrestricted use of the technology has allowed conception to be divorced from marriage and the interests of the child in having both a mother and a father. Increasingly it has been used to give those who want to deny or bypass God's design for human sexuality a way to become a parent. The desire to be a parent is understandable since children enrich our lives, but these technologies, divorced from the benefits a child receives (and needs) from having a married mother and father, makes the focus of childbearing a decision based on the desires of the adult. The child becomes another "thing" people want among the other "things" they want in order to live what they think will be a happier and fuller life.

Several years ago some doctors in Chattanooga, Tennessee, specializing in reproductive technologies put up a billboard. It came down after enough citizens complained. The message was simple and profound and reflective of what has been said: it was a picture of a cute baby with the words, "Want one?" The message, though crassly put, only expressed what abortion had taught us, but apparently when confronted with it a lot of people didn't like it.

The educative aspect of the law has been lost among many Christian lawmakers and lawyers.

The educative aspect of the law has been lost among many Christian lawmakers and lawyers. Several years ago there were a series of incidents in which pregnant teens unceremoniously "dumped" their newborns in dumpsters or otherwise killed them. In response, and out of a desire to save these innocent lives, a number of states began to enact what I call "baby drop off" laws. Pursuant to these laws a mother can drop off her newborn within so many days of birth at certain locations and no questions will be asked. The state will raise the child.

Tennessee passed such a law, and I remember serving on the Senate committee that recommended the proposed law for passage to the full Senate. A district attorney from another state that had been among the first to approve such a law came to testify in support of the law. My exchange with him was demonstrative of our lack of understanding about the educative effect of the law.

I asked the district attorney if he was concerned that, over time, the law would communicate to our young people that a baby is like any other commercial commodity that could be "returned" if one is "not completely happy" with his or her "purchase," and that they could engage in sex without consequences. I asked him that if the law taught those lessons whether we would further erode our sense of life's inherent dignity, which could, in turn, result in more babies dying. His response was that he didn't care about that; he was concerned about saving the lives of the children that might be left in a dumpster over the coming weeks and months.

I agreed that saving the life of such babies was a good and noble act; however, I reminded him that at one time we thought if we made abortion legal and safe that we would have fewer abortions over time, but the result had instead been a debasement of human life such that partial birth abortion had become acceptable.[44]

When we lose sight of the educative effect of the law, we lose sight of the possibility that the action today may produce an even greater harm in the future. With the baby drop off law the majority concluded that the value of saving one life at the moment was worth the risk that even more babies' lives would be lost in the future as respect for the value and dignity of human life continued to diminish.

> **When we lose sight of the educative effect of the law, we lose sight of the possibility that the action today may produce an even greater harm in the future.**

As life has become less valuable in the eyes of the majority of people, there may well come a day when people try to justify abortion on the grounds that the value of unwanted babies' lives are not worth the cost to taxpayers of raising children over the next 20 years.[45] We can't forget that while trying to say that the unwanted baby should be rescued, the baby drop off laws are simultaneously teaching a sexual ethic that is likely to produce even more discarded lives. Maybe the better approach would have been to punish the mother's crime because then the message would have been consistent: the destruction of life requires that justice be meted out to the one who destroyed it.

While many Christians have failed to appreciate the educative aspect of law, not everyone has. In their book, *After the Ball: How America Will Overcome Its Fear and Loathing of Gays in the 90's*, authors Marshall Kirk and Hunter Madsen set forth the steps they thought would have be taken to accomplish the purpose reflected in their book's title. One of the things they said had to happen was a change in the sodomy laws of several states. And here is the reason why:

> Many gays think, because of this lax enforcement [of sodomy laws], that they are getting off lightly; that the system is tolerably lenient. But they are misled. They haven't understood how sodomy laws are intended to function....[T]he survival of gay sodomy laws, even unenforced, sends a message to both straights and gays that homosexuality is intrinsically wrong, sinful because it's "unnatural." And that, really, is the underlying purpose of such laws....

Clearly, the authors' understanding of the educative affect of the law exceeds that of an overwhelming majority of Christians, particularly those in our pulpits who refuse to talk about the political battles related to issues like life and homosexuality.

...we must ask ourselves how well we love our neighbor if we do not care what the law will teach them.

But that brings us back to the larger issue at hand: the law and loving our neighbor. If the law will shape our neighbor's understanding of right and wrong, good and evil, justice and injustice—and it will—then we must ask ourselves how well we love our neighbor if we do not care what the law will teach them.

For example, many in the Christian community would say that they love the young woman in despair over an unplanned pregnancy, and Christians rightly want to come to her aid. To come alongside that young woman is to love her. But how well do we love her if we haven't also cared about whether our public schools are teaching her a view of human sexuality that condones and even at times encourages the promiscuous behavior that may have led to her pregnancy?

We say we care for the poor, but how much do we really love the poor if we accept (and maybe even support) the idea that it is okay for the state, through the lottery, to become the bookie for a gambling operation that more often than not attracts the poor and the money they can scarce afford to lose? And worse yet, it is a state-sanctioned gambling operation that transfers the losses of the poorer among us to those in higher income brackets so that their children can get a better education.

If we really believe that homosexual conduct undermines the humanity of those involved, then how much do we love our neighbor if we allow the law to equate homosexuality with race, sex and national origin, saying it is an "identity," not destructive and immoral behavior.

In each of these instances, the answer comes back to the law written on our hearts: If the law allows something or protects something, then it must be okay, because law would surely not allow, much less protect, what is evil or wrong. How much do we Christians really love our neighbor if we do not resist, let alone advocate for, laws that will teach as good the evil that destroys lives?

Perhaps a word picture will help. Imagine that we live our lives walking along the edge of a cliff. That cliff represents our culture. Every day some people get too close to the edge, and they fall off the cliff. Their lives are broken; some even die. The Christian's natural reaction is to rush to the bottom of the cliff and begin to build clinics and hospitals to heal those whose lives have been broken by the fall. But too often Christians think very little about building a fence at the top that might keep people from falling off in the first place.

If, however, we see law from a biblical perspective as that which is intended to restrain evil, then we will *also* build a fence at the top, even if in doing so we are considered hateful. If we love our neighbors who may be drawn by culture too close to the edge of the cliff, it would be hateful not to have a fence at the top that might save some from falling. I submit that we do not love our neighbor well if we have no concern about whether our laws restrain evil, as God defines that term according to his word. At best, it would seem that we are indifferent to saving or protecting our neighbor from a harm that could have been prevented. Even worse are laws that *protect* what God calls evil, for then we make it easier for our neighbor to be induced into harmful actions and situations.

In response to these thoughts, some will say that standing up for laws that "judge" other people's behavior as wrong is not loving, is intolerant and creates an unloving society. No doubt many whom the law would restrain will see a Christian's actions in support of such laws as unloving. But, again, as Christians, we dare not forget the educative aspect of the law.

The failure to restrain evil, which is an aspect of lawlessness, does not produce a loving (tolerant) culture.

In this regard, I find this statement by Jesus very interesting: "And because lawlessness will abound, the love of many will grow cold."[46] The failure to restrain evil, which is an aspect of lawlessness, does not produce a loving (tolerant) culture. Rather it produces the opposite. I believe it does so because in a lawless environment the focus of the society becomes the individual—who I am and what I want to do. Not surprisingly, we find the name "lawless one" given to Satan, whose focus was so on himself that he sought to exalt himself over God.

Love, on the other hand, is other-centered. It is not self-centered. It finds joy in knowing that God loves it when we look to the welfare of our neighbor. Allowing everything in the name of love is not loving one's neighbor. Rather, biblically speaking, it is actually loving lawlessness, and the end result will be a lack of love. Love will grow cold.

But there is more to the politics of loving our neighbor than supporting laws that reflect God's definition of right and wrong and voting for the politicians who support those laws. It is doing so with a broken and contrite heart. Jesus stood up to the leaders of Israel in his day. He often did not mince words. But his words and actions proceeded from a heart that was broken over the fact his

Allowing everything in the name of love is not loving one's neighbor.

people were lost. In the same chapter in which Jesus tells those listening that they would perish if they did not repent, he is also recorded as saying, "How often I wanted to gather your children together, just as a hen gathers her brood under her wings, and you would not have it!"[47]

We must speak the truth, not in anger, but with hearts broken for those who will perish if they do not "come to the knowledge of the truth."[48] Setting up legal roadblocks to that knowledge is not very loving.

Chapter 9

Putting the Pieces Together

—⁓—

One day after a Senate committee hearing in which I had rigorously questioned a member of our governor's cabinet who had been testifying, a colleague came up to me. She said she had "finally figured out my problem." Thinking she might save me the cost of therapeutic counseling, I asked what she thought it was.

My problem, according to her, was that I "thought people were basically bad when they really were basically good." She then offered to provide me some books to read that summer that would help me see her point and my blind spot. I thanked her and asked if she would be willing to read a book I thought confirmed my perspective. She said yes, and then I told her that she really only needed to read one chapter in the book, Chapter 3 of the Book of Genesis describing the fall of man. She never sent me those books.

That one conversation was a perfect reflection of the fact that one's worldview is critical when it comes to law and government. She rightly recognized that at the root of my governing philosophy was a worldview that distrusted people in power. When it comes to putting all the pieces of the preceding chapters together to determine

> **That one conversation was a perfect reflection of the fact that one's worldview is critical when it comes to law and government.**

what kind of laws we should support, I submit that there are two overarching worldview perspectives from Scripture that a Christian should keep in mind.

A first, broad, general principle in evaluating the propriety of a law is the present, natural condition of mankind. The nature of man was precisely the point of disagreement between my colleague and me. The biblical view of man is that he is fallen. Every law should be evaluated in terms of how it corresponds to the fact that man is fallen.

Whether man is basically good and only does some bad things from time to time, as my colleague thought, or is basically evil and does good things from time to time, is not a distinction without a difference. If we believe a person is basically good, then that can lead to the utopian belief that if we can just change an individual's circumstances or provide enough information or education, then that individual's inherent goodness will be released and come shining through.

That may sound good and offer a sense of much-needed hope in face of the brokenness all around us, but Scripture says just the opposite. Here are a couple of quick points in this regard. First, we are said to be "dead" in our trespasses and sins. Dead men do not have any good in them. They are dead. So, though we live in the physical body, until we are made alive spiritually by the finished work of Christ, we are "slaves to sin."[49] Second, in Romans 7 we learn that even those who are spiritually alive in Christ often know what to do, but they don't do it.

In other words, scripturally speaking, we need to be wary of thinking that education is some kind of panacea. And, even apart from Scripture, experience tells us that this is true because there are a lot of very educated people who do some very horrible things. This doesn't mean that education is unimportant. It is important, but it does mean that it is foolish for us and for policy makers to assume that we can educate people well enough that they will choose to do good all the time. Education alone is not a final solution.

A second basic consideration to keep in mind is really just an aspect of our fallenness. When we evaluate public policies we need to keep in mind what I call the "Adamic Shift." Fallen people tend to do what Adam did when he defended himself against God's inquiry. Adam essentially blamed everybody else for

> **When we evaluate public policies we need to keep in mind what I call the "Adamic Shift."**

his failure. It was Eve's fault because she offered the forbidden fruit to him. But it was not enough just to blame Eve. Adam made a point of reminding God that it was he who had given Eve to him in the first place. It was God's fault too.[50]

The Adamic Shift is a way of describing the fact that fallen man tends to shift blame or shift responsibility to someone else whenever possible. It is not surprising, therefore, that God seeks to discourage that behavior. He does so, in part, by allowing "sluggards" (God's term, not mine) to reap the natural consequences of their sluggardly behavior.[51]

While letting people suffer from their irresponsible behavior seems heartless and helping them out of their mess seems compassionate, removing the natural consequences of wrong actions can actually create a merciless trap. When we know someone else will take responsibility for us, it makes choosing irresponsibility less costly, and if we are not careful, our irresponsible behavior can become habitual. As a consequence, it becomes easy to get trapped in a cycle of irresponsible behavior and dependency on others.

Civil government can actually encourage the Adamic Shift when it tries to ameliorate the consequences of irresponsible behavior. When this happens and the cycle of dependency develops, then civil government fails at one of its primary responsibilities: protecting human liberty. Instead it becomes a purveyor of the bondage that inevitably accompanies dependency.

Getting out of that bondage is not painless, which helps explain why few people who are dependent on the civil government for their basic resources will ever vote to reduce or eliminate the funds or programs upon which they are dependent. And as we are seeing, this is true even though the civil government upon which they are dependent will eventually be bankrupted by excessive debt.[52] No doubt many are willing to allow the debt to pile up because they think they can "shift" the debt problem to the next generation.

While some politicians are quick to point out the immorality of creating dependency and encouraging irresponsibility with respect to individuals, they are not as apt to see that the Adamic Shift also applies to businesses. For example, civil government can encourage this shift when it thinks of some business enterprise as "too large to fail" and steps in to rescue it. A more subtle way of encouraging the Adamic Shift is by subsidizing "important industries" or private not-for-profit organizations that "do good work."

Just as we can encourage bad habits in individuals, subsidization and signaling to entities that we won't let them fail allows costly inefficiencies and bad practices to flourish without consequence. This, in turn, will eventually lead to the kind of economic collapse that costs taxpayers millions and even billions of their hard-earned money. By bailing these entities out or funding their operations, civil government, rather than protecting the property of taxpayers, becomes little more than a thief, taking some people's money to give it to others.

As my Senate colleague noted, there *is* a "problem," but the problem is holding to the wrong worldview. It is not only expensive, it can lead to dependency, loss of freedom and property, and, finally, poverty.

Chapter 10

Lawful Laws

—〰—

So far we have seen that politics and government can be an expression of our love for God and our love for our neighbor. In the last chapter we also looked at a couple of worldview considerations that should undergird our basic thinking. But is that all we Christians can say? Are there no other precepts and principles by which different policies and laws can be evaluated?

To my knowledge, no one, Christian or otherwise, has laid out a foolproof "formula" through which all policies can be evaluated, though John Stuart Mill suggested one.[53] Policy making is not an exact science like mathematics. As referenced in the analysis of Professor Leff's article in Chapter 7, many theories for the evaluation of proposed laws and the regulation of civil conduct have been offered throughout history. Trying to come up with a theory that would never produce, in any situation, a law that no one would consider unjust is a bit like trying to build a secure fortress out of gelatin cubes. It is very unlikely.

Furthermore, no "formula" would produce one set of laws that would work well for all people in all circumstances. John Calvin, acknowledged that the laws of each country would look different.[54] However, to keep law from being only arbitrary, there is value in trying to develop some general principles, grounded in a worldview derived from Scripture, by which Christian citizens and politicians can better determine how to steward the authority of civil government entrusted to them.

In trying to develop some general principles, a word of caution is needed with respect to what follows. The subject of this chapter could itself be an entire book (or a multi-volume treatise). Therefore, what follows is not an exhaustive list of considerations that might apply to the evaluation of a particular public policy. Similarly, no effort has been made to set out general principles that would cover every conceivable type of interaction between people. Instead, the following is a general theory for dealing with the concept of individual rights.[55]

> ...so much of politics today seems to turn on someone's "rights" either being protected or infringed.... individual rights and the denial thereof by another seems to be the primary source of political conflict today.

The reason I have limited this chapter to what I call "individual rights" is because so much of politics today seems to turn on someone's "rights" either being protected or infringed. The assertion of individual rights and the denial thereof by another seems to be the primary source of political conflict today. As my experience with the ACLU advocate demonstrated, it is much easier for all of us to assert rights than it is to identify where those rights come from and what should even qualify as a right. Hopefully, the following will prompt a much-needed discussion in this area instead of being dismissed as "hate speech" by those who disagree with me.

One of the observations in the last chapter is that civil government can be engaged in what really amounts to theft. However, many today would no doubt say that the civil government can't steal (or do any kind of moral wrong) because it makes the law. To them it is circular reasoning to think the law can somehow break the law. In fact, this kind of thinking—that the law just is what it is—dominates current legal thought and instruction, but Scripture rebukes this kind of modern day wrong thinking about law.

In 1 Timothy 1:8-9 we read:

> We know that the law is good if one uses it lawfully, knowing this: that the law is not made for a righteous person, but for the lawless and insubordinate, for the ungodly and for sinners.

While the text is referring to the way in which the words of the laws governing the Hebrew nation were interpreted to avoid the spirit of the law, there is at the root of the text the notion that law can be used "lawfully" and, presumably, "unlawfully." What could this mean as we apply the principle in the context of civil laws? And how does it relate to the modern thinking that law just "is" and that a law properly adopted "makes" something lawful or legal, right or wrong? In my view, the verse means exactly what it says: a law can be used unlawfully and that doing so is not good. The verse also gives us some guidance as to what it means for a law to be used unlawfully.

First, for a law to be used lawfully from a biblical perspective it should be directed at restraining or punishing the lawless and the ungodly. If it is not, then the law is not being used properly. This is consistent with what has previously been said. Second, a parallel principle also is true. For a law to be used lawfully it should not be used to restrain the righteous. If it is, then it is not being used lawfully.[56] Third, the verse at least seems to imply what was said in our earlier discussion, namely that law should encourage what is good and punish what is evil. A law is not substantively "good" simply because it is the law. If the law affirms as good what Scripture says is evil or restrains or punishes what the Scripture affirms as good, then the law is not being used lawfully. In other words, a civil law must conform to or be consistent with God's higher law. Fourth, the verse also seems to strike a blow to the idea that the ends can justify the means. We cannot use the law in wrong ways in order to achieve some good desired end.

> **...there is such a thing as a bad law, *even if it is properly enacted*.**

In other words, there is such a thing as a bad law, *even if it is properly enacted*. Have you ever supported a change to, or the repeal of, an existing law? If so, then you have tacitly said that the law on the books, as it is, is not a good law, *even if it was properly enacted as a matter of procedure*. We do not advocate for a change in a law that we think is good. We all know that not all laws are substantively good.

Putting these various thoughts together we can conclude that a law must be substantively good: encouraging what God calls good and restraining or punishing what God calls evil. And it must be used lawfully: it should be directed at wrongdoers and not do wrong in the name of doing good.[57] Thus we have to wrestle with two questions. The first is: "How do you encourage the good without, in the process, doing wrong?" The second is the other side of the coin: "How do you restrain what is wrong without, in the process, doing wrong?" If we don't answer both of these questions correctly, then all kinds of evil can be justified in the name of doing good.

Protecting Rights Without Doing Wrong

With the foregoing as a starting place for our discussion of individual rights, let's consider the Ten Commandments. There are several reasons for doing so.

First, even most non-Christians have no problem with those commandments related to man's relationship to, and interactions with, his fellow man, even though these commands are frequently violated by all of us:

Honor your mother and father (the fifth commandment)

Do not murder (the sixth commandment)

Do not commit adultery (the seventh commandment)

Do not steal (the eighth commandment)

Do not bear false witness (the ninth commandment)[58]

Second, the Ten Commandments give us a basis for rights that is fixed because the commands flow from and are consistent with the immutable nature and character of God. These commands should provide a solid starting place for discussion within the Christian community, unless, of course, we want to reject the Ten Commandments or rationalize them away. For the non-Christian, this may not be a very satisfactory basis for a right, but it is at least as satisfactory as faulty human reason, the tyranny of majority rule or the corruptibility of sheer power.

> ...the Ten Commandments give us a basis for rights that is fixed because the commands flow from and are consistent with the immutable nature and character of God.

Third, for the Christian, the moral law of God, outlined in the Ten Commandments, could be viewed as an example or model of what law should and should not do. God anticipated that other nations would recognize the wisdom of the law he gave Israel. Moses, in recounting the law of God that included the Ten Commandments, tells the people of Israel that "the peoples who will hear all these statutes" will look at the functioning of Israel under those statutes and "say, 'Surely this great nation is a wise and understanding people.'"[59] In other words, governing *and* living according to God's law was something other nations would see and look up to in admiration. God anticipated that his law would be a "model" for others. And it would be unreasonable to think that God would give us a set of basic laws that violated his own standards for law.[60]

If, therefore, we take God's moral law as a cue for the development of our own laws, we again see that the law is mostly negative: directed at restraining or prohibiting evil. For example, in contrast to the commandment, "do not murder," God did not affirmatively say "cherish, value and respect life, even to the point of loving the person it would be easy to hate and you might even want to kill." Similarly, God's law did not affirmatively say "love your spouse," "give of your possessions to others in need" or "always tell the whole truth." Those are, however, the volitional, affirmative aspects or, we might say, the positive side of the negative "do not's" of these laws. In other words, the Ten Commandments set a threshold of behavior below which man and society must not go, but love, which underlies the volitional, positive side of the law, goes beyond what the law requires.[61]

But notice something else: the fact that each commandment prohibits a certain action means that when a commandment is broken, a right of another person has been violated. In other words, there is a flip-side to the admonitions and prohibitions in the Ten Commandments. A person has a right to have his marital and parental relationships respected and upheld, to have his life protected, to securely possess his property and to expect honesty in his dealings with others. These rights we might call the "positive rights" of individuals.

In addition to helping us identify the positive rights of individuals, we must remember that prohibiting the violation of those rights by means of punishment actually encourages and promotes what is good. For example, no law can make a person honest; however, civil government, by punishing dishonesty, can encourage honesty, the volitional, positive value upon which the prohibition on dishonestly is based. In time, more people are likely to be honest because dishonesty becomes so disreputable and unacceptable.[62] And notice that this means of encouraging what is good (honesty) by restraining what is evil (lying) does not violate another person's positive rights, an issue we will subsequently address.

> ...the fact that each commandment prohibits a certain action means that when a commandment is broken, a right of another person has been violated.

But one more thing needs to be understood regarding positive rights before the picture is complete. While it might seem obvious to most, it is worth stating that there is no affirmative or positive right to do wrong. The law must not protect any so-called right to do wrong.[63] In a sense, it is a corollary to the prohibition on using the law unlawfully.

For example, I have a positive right to expect honesty and fair dealing in my relationships, but I do not have a right to lie to and be dishonest with others. I have the positive right to possess my property, but I do not have the right to dispossess others of their property. I have the positive right to have my life protected, but I do not have the right to take another's life, except in defense of my own life.[64] I have the positive right to have my relationship with my spouse and my children respected, but I do not have the right to interfere in or prohibit another man and woman from entering into a marital relationship.[65]

Putting the foregoing thoughts together, we arrive at the following general principles. First, the law cannot be used to make a person righteous, but it can be used to administer justice when a positive right of another is violated. Second, because the law cannot do harm in order to do good, the law cannot by its own terms violate the positive rights of another. Thus, if a law can protect the positive right of one person without violating the positive rights of another, then it may be seen as a good law.[66]

In this situation, the person who violates such a law violates the positive rights of another, and that person can be punished or restrained as a matter of justice. Punishing the wrongdoer does him no wrong for two reasons. First, the wrongdoer had no positive right to do wrong. And second, the very notion of justice means that the wrongdoer must in some way either be restrained or made to make restitution. If the positive rights of a person who violates the positive rights of another can never be "violated," then justice in the form of restraint or restitution could never be had. In essence, the act of doing wrong to another person operates as a forfeiture of the wrongdoer's rights to the extent justice requires. But justice also requires that the wrongdoer's rights not be diminished or taken away beyond what justice requires. This is the principle of proportionality found in the Scripture whereby for an eye taken, an eye shall be required of the wrongdoer, not his head.

These general principles and this restriction on the power of civil government should serve to protect our positive rights to the greatest degree possible while simultaneously according us the greatest degree of individual liberty.[67]

Chapter 11

The Politics of Loving God and Loving My Neighbor

—ɯɯ—

Tennessee's Democratic lieutenant governor and Speaker of the Senate leaned over my desk on the Senate floor and put his arm around me. He needed a favor from the Republican whom he had named chairman of one of the Senate's standing committees. In that moment, I was forced to determine what I really believed. My "crisis" arose out of the fact that, during his recently completed campaign, the lieutenant governor had promised two different people that he would appoint them to a commission. The problem was that only one position was open. So he had proposed a bill to expand the number of people on the commission. But the bill had failed in committee, the committee I chaired.

Now, near the close of the legislative session, the lieutenant governor wanted to have the bill presented to the committee one more time to see if he could get a different result. The problem was that the committee had closed for the year, subject to the call of the chairman. While, as chairman, I could call the committee back into session, the Senate rules prevented a bill that had not passed in committee from being reconsidered unless a majority of the committee members signed a letter to the chairman asking that the bill be reheard. I had received no such letter, thus the lieutenant governor's visit to my desk.

What the lieutenant governor wanted me to do was to be a good team player and help him out. I wanted to be a good team player. The question was, "What team was I on?" There were several from which to choose:

- The "team" composed of those whom the lieutenant governor had made committee chairs: the "lieutenant governor's team;"

- The "team" composed of Republicans who might benefit from or at least enjoy seeing the Democratic lieutenant governor squirm and perhaps alienate one of his constituents and campaign supporters;

- The "team" composed of the members of my committee who looked to me for leadership; or

- The "team" called the "Senate" that had adopted rules by which the Senate was to operate.

I told him I appreciated having been named a committee chair, but it was my duty as chairman and part of my oath to follow the rules of order that had been established. Since I didn't have the requisite letter, I couldn't reopen the committee. His parting words were to remind me in a very firm way that he had put me where I was and I was not being loyal or a good team player.

The story illustrates the very nub of the issue related to the "politics" of loving God and loving our neighbor. As Christians we have to first determine on whose team we are. It will determine how we "play the game."

Over the years I've come to see the truth of what we find throughout Scripture: it is what we do as Christians rather than what we say that provides the real clue as to what we believe. What we do reveals on whose team we are, and we are either on God's team or we are not. And in my experience, it seems that nothing better reveals whose team we are on than what we really believe about who is in control: God or man. Saying God is in control is easy. Living out life on the basis of that premise is what is hard.

Based on my observations of others *and* myself in the context of politics over a number of years, I have come to believe that, as a practical matter, the answer more often than not is that many of us who profess to be Christians don't really believe God is in control. Whom we really believe to be in control in any

> ...many of us who profess to be Christians don't really believe God is in control.

particular situation is often indicated by the degree to which we are fearful, anxious and insecure or peaceful, calm and confident.

What we fear reveals who or what we value or reverence the most.[68] None of us fears the loss or destruction of what is not valuable to us. What we fear losing most is what we value most. As Christians, we either fear God most or we fear something or someone else. In those moments we find ourselves fearing something or someone else, that has become our god. When that "something" is our god, then there is no real help for us. That means we have no choice but to be responsible for ensuring our continued relationship to that thing. Since we are on our own, we wind up having to save our god.

In the rest of this chapter we will examine this issue of control from the perspective of the elected official, the minister and the Christian citizen.

Elected Official

Perhaps the best way to demonstrate what I mean relative to the elected official is by example. On more than one occasion in my last years in the Tennessee Senate I heard someone ask me prior to a vote how I thought the vote would look in a campaign mail piece. I admit that the thought crossed my mind at times. However, in that moment, the elected official must ask himself if he is trying to be "wise" and "prudent" or if he really believes that voters alone are in control of who holds political office as opposed to God?

On another occasion, I was walking back to my legislative office with a couple of my colleagues after being on the losing end of a vote in committee. I asked them if I was wrong about the principle I had advocated in committee because, by taking the position opposite mine, they seemed to disagree. The answer was something along the lines of "probably not but you just can't vote against" the special interest group that was supporting the bill. In that instance, by taking that position the elected official apparently believes it is an organization or the voters represented by that organization that is in control of who holds office, not God.[69]

In both of these instances, when it comes to who is in control, mighty King Nebuchadnezzar would have reminded us, as elected officials, that God ultimately decides who holds power and authority within the governmental process. As the psalmist said, "For exaltation [comes] neither from the east nor from the west nor from the south. But God [is] the Judge: He puts down one, And exalts another. "[70]

I also remember a sponsor of a bill in the Tennessee House telling me several years ago that a committee hearing on a bill he was presenting had been stopped in order for the person who was then Speaker of the House to meet with the committee chairman, appointed by the Speaker. The purpose of the meeting? It was to let the committee chairman know that he would be removed as chairman before the day was out if he supported a certain version of the bill. A version of the bill, watered down by amendment, was voted out of committee later that day.

In that situation, the thing the election official values most is his committee assignment. Since those assignments are made by the Speaker or chairman of that legislative body, then the elected official who most prizes his committee assignments will naturally worry about how the Speaker or chairman perceives his actions. This is the person who is really perceived to be in control. Thus, the elected official must keep that person happy.

> ...whether one is effective or not, and more importantly, what the meaning of effectiveness is, must be viewed from the perspective of the team upon which that person is "playing" and who is in control on the team.

The desire to be "effective" also tends to reveal who an elected official believes to be in control and who is his god. There is nothing wrong with wanting to be effective, but often the hidden motivation is the elected official's reputation in the eyes of others. In that case, the elected official's god is his reputation.

Similar to the situation involving committee assignments, elected officials who want to be "effective" are often fearful of bucking the leadership. The fear is that leadership will intentionally frustrate the elected official's agenda as a means of "getting him back in line." Then the legislator, unable to get anything done, is more likely to be seen by his constituents as "ineffective." Here the subtle lie of the devil is that one's effectiveness depends on having the support of the leadership. However, whether one is effective or not, and more importantly, what the meaning of effectiveness is, must be viewed from the perspective of the team upon which that person is "playing" and who is in control on the team.

For example, a newly appointed chairman of a legislative committee, a fellow Christian, once declined to sponsor a potentially controversial bill that I had brought to him. In declining to sponsor the bill he said he was trying to figure out how best to help on issues like this. He was concerned that he couldn't "help" if he made himself ineffective. But it seemed to me (and I pray I was wrong) that what he was really concerned with was whether leadership would be upset with him if he sponsored the bill and whether that would make him ineffective (or perhaps the concern was whether it would cost him his chairmanship at some point).

Respecting those whom God has placed in leadership over a legislator is legitimate but it can become easy for a legislator to rationalize a desire to be effective and lose sight of the fact that, ultimately, God makes a legislator effective. "Apart from me," Jesus said, "you can do nothing."[71] Pleasing leadership does not always make a legislator effective in God's eyes and if he or she is not careful leadership becomes the "god" the legislator wants to please.[72]

It is as if there is a political way of doing things and a biblical way of doing things, and the biblical way does not apply to politics.

Unfortunately, upon hearing such examples, some may just shrug and say, "Well, that's just politics." But think for a moment about the assumption behind such a statement. The statement assumes that there is this thing called "politics," it operates by its own rules, and God is just not really relevant. It is as if there is a political way of doing things and a biblical way of doing things, and the biblical way does not apply to politics. Such thinking is the kind of unbiblical compartmentalization we discussed in Chapter 5.

There are also those who will say that politics is the art of the possible. What is usually meant is this: in politics, every member of a certain elected body has the same right to vote as every other member and sometimes the members do come to loggerheads. At that point, it is often said an elected official does not so much what he wants as what is possible. Sometimes doing what is possible is the right thing. But sometimes doing nothing is the right thing! Knowing which circumstance is which is often a difficult question for the elected official.

For instance, in Tennessee, under our state constitution, we must pass a balanced budget. So, when it comes to the budget, Tennessee legislators cannot just agree to disagree. And unlike a business with a chief executive officer who can make the final call, one legislator cannot decide for all the others what budget needs to be passed. Compromise, in this case, can become a constitutional necessity.[73]

But there are tougher situations. Consider the not so hypothetical case of abortion. There are those who believe abortion is murder, period. For them abortion should not be allowed even in cases of rape and incest. But if there are currently no laws restricting abortion, is it wrong to support a compromise bill that would at least make all abortions illegal other than those for rape and incest or to save the life of the mother?

Some would say, "Of course. The proposed law would reduce abortions and move closer to the goal of banning abortion." That is true, but sometimes the decision is not so easy. There may be other factors at play. Let me share with you a real example of one of the "other factors" that can come into play and a principle that I think can be drawn from it.

In 2000, Tennessee's state Supreme Court "found" a fundamental right to abortion in the state's constitution and struck down as unconstitutional Tennessee's abortion-specific informed consent and waiting period laws.[74] For years a House subcommittee killed a proposed constitutional amendment that would reverse the court's ruling and once again make the constitution silent on the issue, allowing abortion to be regulated to the extent permitted under the rulings of the U.S. Supreme Court.

The inability to get the legislature to put the amendment on the ballot on our first several attempts was not as simple as "we'll get 'em next year." In Tennessee, citizens can only vote on constitutional amendments during a gubernatorial election, which occurs once every four years. If the legislature can't get an amendment passed to go on the ballot for the upcoming gubernatorial election, then the whole process has to start over with a view toward getting the amendment on the ballot four years later!

The problem the legislature had in getting the amendment through the House was the committee that first had to approve the bill was made up of strongly pro-abortion representatives. The members of the committee were appointed by the strongly pro-abortion Speaker of the House. The Speaker of the House was selected by a majority of the majority party. And that majority was pro-abortion.

Thus, there were only two ways by which the full House would ever be able to vote on the proposed amendment. The first was to make a procedural motion on the House floor to bring the amendment out of the committee and directly to the floor. Unfortunately, this kind of motion had to be approved by two-thirds of the representatives who voted on the motion. Getting two-thirds of the vote seemed unlikely though I have learned that you never know how legislators will vote once they are forced to cast a vote. The other way was for the minority party to pick up five seats in the next election and hope the new majority party would elect a pro-life Speaker. Hopefully, a new pro-life Speaker would ensure that the key committee had a majority of pro-life members. However, waiting for and hoping for a favorable election result meant that the process would be delayed at least another four years.

However, one of the pro-life legislators in the minority party came up with an ingenious "plan" by which the amendment might get to the House floor. There was a risk though. Some members of the majority party targeted for defeat in the next election might have been able to protect themselves from being attacked on the abortion issue during the upcoming campaign. If those targeted legislators voted for the plan, but there were not enough votes to get the amendment to the floor, then those legislators could not be attacked for not being pro-life. They would have voted for the pro-life plan.

The night before the plan was to be offered and voted upon, I sat in the office of the representative who had devised the plan. We were going over anticipated procedural objections and developing responses. An influential member of his political party came in and requested that he consider not asking for a vote on his plan. The reason was, as just described, to avoid giving some members of the majority party "political cover." Politically speaking, the request was one we would expect, as it seemed reasonable enough.

The request seemed reasonable because the odds were that the plan would not get the necessary number of votes anyway. And if the targeted legislators could not be defeated in the next election because their vote for the plan took the abortion issue out of the upcoming campaign, then the existing majority party likely would remain in control. That meant the speakership would remain pro-abortion. That meant we'd fare no better in getting the amendment on the ballot in four years than we had over the current four years period. Under that scenario, all would be lost. The amendment would not get to the floor for a vote and control of the House would not change from pro-abortion to pro-life.

However, the representative and I concluded that the possibility that someday another party would take control of the House did not justify allowing babies to die for several more years if, by God's grace, we could get the votes the next morning that were needed. We decided to do what we thought was the right thing on the immediate issue before us: vote on the representative's plan. It was the one issue that we could "control." We realized we could not "control" what happened in future elections, and so we decide to let that more distant issue take care of itself.

The sponsor went forward the next morning. The plan did not get enough votes and failed. And, as predicted by the person the night before, one of the primary targets in the upcoming election voted for the plan. He now had the political cover that was supposed to make him harder to beat. Without his defeat, *along with that of a few others*, a change in control of the House was not likely. All appeared lost at the time.

But a funny thing happened on election day. The targeted candidate lost anyway. So did a few of the majority party's other candidates, one of whom was chided multiple times during the campaign for voting for some of the procedural efforts designed to kill the plan. That candidate's defeat helped provide *the one vote margin* by which control of the House changed hands! The thing that wasn't going to happen if the plan failed happened anyway.

The lesson I learned was this: beware of compromising to a position that is "better than nothing" if the reason is to achieve a purely political end, such as setting up a political opponent or saving one's own skin politically. When that becomes the reason for compromise, then the goal of the legislation in question and the purpose of compromise is no longer to advance the substantive ethical good. Rather, the goal is to advance a purely political good. In that case, compromise means sacrificing the potential ethical good for a potential political good. For me at least, the underlying assumption for compromise in this situation is a false belief that I need to take political matters into my own hands, and doing that means that I just can't quite trust God with the results.

This is not the same as supporting the greatest amount of progress toward some substantive, ethical good when not doing so would otherwise result in no substantive or ethical good or progress being made at all. More times than not, it would seem that the incremental approach is preferable to nothing. However, there are some who would protest this incremental approach.

Often the argument of those who oppose the incremental approach is that by achieving only a limited good *the political pressure* needed to reach the ultimate good is lost. That is a reasonable thought.[75] But I refer to my previous example. What might be in the future is up to God. And while there is nothing wrong *per se* with being politically smart, we need to be careful that our political thinking doesn't turn into manipulative thinking. Manipulative thinking is tantamount to saying that God needs our help and he doesn't.

> **"Are you kidding? I understand politics. I've been a church deacon and choir director!"**

This treatise is all well and good as it relates to elected officials, but most people will never hold elected office. So for the rest of us, what does the "politics of loving God" mean? Let's look at it from the perspective of the minister and then church members.

Ministers

When I ran for office, I was often asked what qualified me for elected office since I was a political novice. My answer was simple: "Are you kidding? I understand politics. I've been a church deacon and choir director!" Everyone laughed because they knew exactly what I meant—I had grappled with trying to figure out how to do the right thing without making everybody in the church mad at me or losing my job. And after all, isn't that what we think most politicians try to do—make as many people happy and as few unhappy as is possible so they can keep their jobs?

Let's not kid ourselves when we say we don't want politics in the church. Some forms of "politics" already are in the church. But when it comes to the politics of public policy, my experience tells me that many (though not all) ministers avoid it like the devil. For the minister, "the politics of loving God" will mean coming into conflict with "the politics of the church."

For the minister, "the politics of loving God" will mean coming into conflict with "the politics of the church."

What is hard about the politics of loving God, as has been described, is that it requires worrying less about the effect of bringing "politics" into the church and more about whether the members under the minister's charge know how to love God and their neighbor well by faithfully stewarding the political authority they have been given. Are pastors willing to encourage sound stewardship in the realm of politics and leave the results to God? If so, ministers must do more than urge their church members to vote. At the very least they must equip them with an understanding of the basic biblical principles by which they can evaluate a proposed public policy or a candidate for office and then encourage them to take appropriate action.

This is not easy. I realize that in doing this the minister can face personal concerns about continued "employment." It is natural that such a thought would enter a minister's mind, but it raises the question of who is in control. Is it God, or is it the person in the pew, or the board of deacons or elders? I fear that the real answer, based on the silence in so many churches on issues touching politics, is that the minister fears the person in the pew or the lay leaders more than God.[76]

Not too long ago I had a conversation with a minister that left me wondering if this question wasn't in the back of his mind. As we talked about the need to address political and cultural issues, he said he agreed with me, but he lamented the fact that his elders had bought the modern-day version of the separation of church and state. I tried to encourage him that, as their minister, he might want to consider taking time to teach them otherwise. This, of course, entailed risk[77] because the elders might not prove very teachable and in his denomination, the elders hold the power to recommend that his call as minster not be renewed.

While I am not a minister charged with leading a local congregation, I can appreciate the minister's situation. It is easy to rationalize not doing something that could be controversial in order to protect our personal (and financial) well-being as well as that of our family. It is not unlike the internal, spiritual examination that I had to undergo all the time as an elected official: Was it up to me to keep myself in office or was that God's problem? Even now, as the leader of an organization that depends upon financial contributions to pay the bills, I find it easy to wonder if donors will perceive something I do in such a way that they stop donating. But the question for all of us still remains: Is God really in control?

Are pastors willing to encourage sound stewardship in the realm of politics and leave the results to God?

Interestingly, the preceding paragraph reflects the very subtlety of the problem. Re-read it with attention to the word "depend." I really want to believe all the time that I do not "depend" on donors to pay the bills, but on God. Thus, the rationalizations with which I have had to deal are not dissimilar from those of the minister. I cannot throw stones, but if you are a minister, I invite you to join me in the struggle to totally trust God.

Let us mutually encourage one another to be honest with others and ourselves about this before him.

Another question a minister might face, related to the first, is what will happen to the numerical size of the church if controversial subjects are raised. No minister likes to preside over a dwindling congregation. But numerical size is only a measure of numerical size. It is mostly relevant to the amount of space needed and the size of the budget. The real issue is this: does numerical growth depend on teaching that is easy on the listeners because it avoids controversial subjects[78] or does it depend on God? These questions point out whom we really depend upon, and the answer depends on whom we believe is really in control.

Another concern I have heard expressed is that touching on these controversial subjects will keep people from being saved. Illustrative of this concern is a conversation I once had with a minister in the Calvinist tradition. He is perhaps one of the most gracious men I have ever met, meek and gentle in both spirit and demeanor. As we discussed talking about the political and cultural issues of the day within the church, he told me that he didn't like to speak of those things, because he was concerned that it would turn someone away from hearing the gospel. Leaving aside the issue of whether the gospel embraces every area of life, including the political, and therefore should be taught, I told him what I thought I had heard him really say.

What I thought I had heard him say was that even though a Calvinist would say he believed in the irresistible grace of God, he really believed that he had the power by his words in the pulpit to prevent God from saving the elect. I tried to encourage him not to consider a person's church attendance, or lack thereof, as proof of the person's eternal state. I reminded him that the offending sermon might be the very sermon that provides the spark the Holy Spirit uses in another place and at a different time to bring about the person's salvation.

As with the elected official, the issue really is who is in control. In this case, it is often a question of who is really in control of the welfare of the church and of the minister's finances. Is it God or is it the minister, the people in the pews or the church's leadership. A minister who is not fully convinced that it is God will find the politics of loving him hard.

The Christian Citizen

For the person in the pew, the "politics of loving God" means risking loss out in the world. While a minister faces the possibility of loss of support among the church's leaders and even loss of employment, there is a sense in which a layperson's situation is much harder. At least the minister is presumably standing for the truth among those who are ostensibly there because they want to hear the truth. The layperson in his neighborhood and at work is not usually in such a potentially friendly place.

The threat of loss is very real for the layperson. Increasingly, the news is filled with reports of Christians losing their jobs or positions because they have essentially been "too Christian" in the

> **Increasingly, the news is filled with reports of Christians losing their jobs or positions because they have essentially been "too Christian" in the marketplace.**

marketplace. I have personally experienced that loss.[79] The threat of such loss makes being involved in politics increasingly risky. It makes the politics of loving God hard.

The fear of loss, economic or otherwise, can motivate us to do things that, when looked at honestly, raise a question about whom we really think is our provider. Not too long ago, I had a conversation with a Christian friend whose spouse belonged to a certain organization that espoused very liberal political positions. He asked why I had supported legislation earlier that year that the organization had opposed. He rightly perceived that a primary purpose of the legislation was to weaken the organization politically.

It was a fair question. My answer was that the organization had great political influence and had repeatedly used it to support sexual promiscuity, abortion, homosexual conduct[80] and other values that undermined God's design for the family. He agreed with me about those issues and their importance, but his response was that they just felt like his wife needed to belong to the organization. She needed to be a member and for it to stay strong in order to protect her rights and income as a member of the profession represented by the organization.

As I said earlier, I understand the struggle with worry and the desire to keep one's job. But I told my friend that what I heard him really saying was that employment security and financial provision depended on the strength of an organization that advanced unrighteousness rather than on God. He had not thought of it that way. Happily, I was able to remind him that years before, when his wife had lost her job and was not a member of any organization, she had received multiple job offers within days. She never missed a paycheck. God had provided without the aid of any support organization.

Here are two other potentially problematic situations: 1) supporting policies that redistribute wealth by actively taking someone else's money in order to subsidize one's industry or profession and 2) supporting the more passive redistributive policy of giving one's business or profession a tax or regulatory break that others don't get. It is hard not to support policies by which one is benefitted personally. After all, giving up or not getting those "advantages" could negatively impact the financial health of one's industry or profession. But the question that must be asked is whether we really support such policies because we see them as our source of provision and security. We may be looking more to the government for provision and security than to God. And if we get honest with ourselves and consider such policies to be government-sanctioned theft, then it may be that our trust in God's provision is so small that we are willing to resort to stealing to secure our personal welfare.

Concluding Thoughts

The bottom line for all of us is a couple of haunting questions:

Who do we believe is in control?

Who is our provider and source of security?[81]

As politics by intimidation becomes increasingly frequent, Christians will have to decide how they will answer those questions. And as Christians in a world that is increasingly hostile to religiously informed values, you and I are going to have to become less concerned with the negative consequences that may flow from standing up for biblical values and for those candidates who support them and more concerned with the knowledge that God sees our obedience as a demonstration of our love for Him and for our neighbor.

But there is one other thing that we will all have to be careful not to use to rationalize our silence in addition to our desire to protect ourselves against the loss of jobs, money or relationships. I have already mentioned it as an issue a minister must address. It will be easy for all of us to want to rationalize staying quiet, because we think that making people mad at us will surely turn people off to Christianity. Maybe so, at least with respect to their understanding of what Americanized Christianity, in general, has become to them with its media campaigns, flashy concert-style services, and self-help-don't-talk-about-sin programs with a God-flavored twist.[82]

But we all know that the early church didn't grow exponentially because of the techniques we now use to promote and present our services and programs. It grew mostly because of its witness—the witness of the early Christians' love for one another and their willingness to accept the suffering their Savior said would be theirs.

> **It will be easy for all of us to want to rationalize staying quiet, because we think that making people mad at us will surely turn people off to Christianity.**

So that led me to think: *Is it not also possible today that our willingness to suffer scorn, ridicule and other types of loss might just cause some to ask, "Can I know this God whom you find to be of such supreme worth that you are willing to lose in this life whatever the majority calls valuable?"* That loss could point them to him and to the possibility of a vital relationship with him rather than to an organization with aesthetically pleasing buildings, entertaining services and programs to become a better person. It just might point people to a way to be free from the bondage of needing to have the approval of other people on everything from the labels on their jeans to the type of cars they drive and the size of houses they inhabit. But, after all, isn't that what Christians should be doing anyway: pointing people to the Truth so that they can experience the even greater eternal pleasure of knowing the God who made them?

Chapter 12

Not a Theocracy, but the Kingdom of God

—ɯ—

People who speak and write like I do inevitably encounter people who are convinced that we intend to usher in some form of a theocratic civil government. I want to confront this concern, because for many Christians, *including me*, the prospect of a theocratic form of civil government is very unsettling. Israel was a theocracy; America is not and should not become one.

I hope that allows you to put any concerns you may have about a theocracy or theocratic form of civil government aside. However, if you need further assurance that I am not recommending a theocracy, think of it this way. Do you, like me, believe engagement in politics is an act of stewardship before God? Do you, like me, believe part of stewarding well the authority God has entrusted to us in the civil realm is honoring the jurisdictional boundaries He has established for civil government and between civil government and the church? If so, then we are on the same page.

That being said, why does my writing cause some kind of "red flag" of concern about a theocracy to pop for so many Christians? I think it is because they hear other people refer to someone like me as a "theonomist," and then they wrongly assume a theonomist believes in a theocratic form of civil government. After all, the words sound a lot alike. Unfortunately, they confuse the term "theocracy" with the term "theonomy." They think each is simply a variation of the other as if they both mean the same thing. But to my way of thinking they don't.

To most people a theocracy is the same thing as a state church or the pope (or some other church leader) being the head of state and using their position to "make" people become Christians. Or it means some kind of immediate rule of the people by God as opposed to God's rule being mediated through the people themselves. But the term "theonomy" does not mean that. What I have described is not a theocratic *view of civil government* but a theonomistic *view of the world*. You will quickly see that they are different, and all Christians, even if they don't realize it, are theonomists.

The best way to understand the concept of theonomy, as distinguished from the kind of theocracy described above, is to look at what the word theonomy means. Just looking at the word helps us get past all the confusion between theocracy and theonomy. The word theonomy is made up of two Greek words: "theos" and "nomos." These are the Greek words for "God" and "law," respectively. In other words, God has established laws by which his universe operates.

This concept is even better understood when we consider it in light of its opposite: autonomy. The word autonomy is made up of two Greek words: "auto" and "nomos." These words mean "self" and, as before, "law." In other words, I am a law unto myself. I make up the law that governs my universe.[83] That is the view of law and the world analyzed by Professor Leff. Most secular legal scholars embrace some variation of that view.

If we think back to our discussion in Chapter 7 of Professor Leff's conclusion about the source of law, we will see that what he rejected was a theonomistic view of law and civil government, and he arrived at a dead end. He could not find a basis for law that didn't have each of us shouting at the other, "Who says?" If the Christian, reacting negatively to the word theocracy, rejects the different concept entailed in the word theonomy, then he or she will arrive at the same conclusion as Professor Leff. The point is that we will operate civil government and enact laws either on the basis of a theonomistic or autonomistic worldview. Looking over time at what kind of cultures have been produced by a legal system grounded on God as the source of law as compared to that which was produced by a man-centered view of law (the autonomous self), then the overall results point positively toward a theonomistic approach.[84]

If we think of the concept of theonomy in terms of God's having established laws that govern the universe, then the thought of a theonomy is not too hard to grasp and is not quite so controversial. We all appreciate the concept of this kind of law when we speak of the laws governing the physical sciences such as gravity, thermodynamics, inertia, etc. But because we stuffed God in a box up on a shelf in the supernatural realm and left the ground floor of nature free of him, we have tended to forget that there are moral laws that govern our universe.

> **But because we stuffed God in a box up on a shelf in the supernatural realm and left the ground floor of nature free of him, we have tended to forget that there are moral laws that govern our universe.**

Of course, as we discussed in Chapter 6, everyone who advocates for a particular policy really knows there are moral laws because they invoke them to insist that their view of that policy is morally right. Our actions are telltale signs that we all do know we are governed by moral laws, and for purposes of this book and this chapter, that is all I mean.

For the Christian who can accept this approach to the issue of theonomy, there is one other thing that must be added. It is an understanding of the kingdom of God. Many Christians who don't get turned back by the alleged "wall of separation" or turned off by my explanation of theonomy, will nevertheless get heartburn over the thought that someone thinks politics can usher in the kingdom of God. I do not believe politics can do that. But the subject of the kingdom of God is one that a book like this must consider.

> ...everyone who advocates for a particular policy really knows there are moral laws because they invoke them

I estimate that as of the date of this writing, I have heard more than 3,000 sermons in a church setting, yet I cannot recall one sermon, let alone a series of sermons, on the subject of the kingdom of God, particularly as it relates to this present life. The closest I have come to hearing any discussion about the meaning of the kingdom of God during a church-based program[85] and its relevance to culture was more or less in passing when someone was speaking of it in the negative, such as I've described: we can't usher in the kingdom of God through politics. But they never really did define what it was that we couldn't usher in through politics. I hope my experience is an extremely isolated one, but given the number of churches and denominations I have passed through, I am sure I am not alone.

I find this void in teaching very interesting since the phrase "kingdom of God" is used 52 times in the synoptic Gospels. Most of the time the words came from the lips of Jesus. In fact, during his last 40 days on earth, the relatively short period between Jesus' resurrection and ascension, we might expect Jesus to emphasize the things his disciples most needed to remember and understand. What did he talk about? He spent his time with them "speaking of the things pertaining to the kingdom of God."[86] If Jesus thought it was this important, you would think we would spend more time trying to understand it. Here is my layman's attempt to explain it. And, again, I'm going to try to keep things simple and leave it to trained theologians to complicate matters.

I like to think of the kingdom of God as being a little like the 4 X 100 medley relay swimming event in the Olympics. The medley relay consists of different swimmers each swimming a different stroke (back, butterfly, breast and free). Each swimmer's stroke contributes to the win by the swimmer functioning well in the three major components of each leg of the race: getting off the blocks, the stroke, and the flip turns. The medley relay will most likely not be won if the swimmers are only good at their particular stroke. If the swimmers are poor at getting off the blocks or make slow turns, their team will not win at the Olympic level, no matter how good they are once they are in the water and in-between the two walls.

And so it is with the kingdom of God. The kingdom of God encompasses all of reality. You might say it is the medley relay race itself. But even as the race has different strokes, all that constitutes our reality has its constituent parts as well. These "parts" were described as "spheres" by Dutch theologian and former prime minister, Abraham Kuyper. Those spheres are sometimes described as family, church and state. Some might speak of the spheres of reality in terms of governing units: the sphere of self-government, family government, ecclesiastical government and civil government. Some might include among the spheres a social sphere, which would consist of things like art, education, science, communication, economics, business, etc. Though some might disagree, I don't think it is particularly important how we divide them up so long as we recognize that there are different spheres with certain functions operating within the created order.

Now let's take this thought and tie it to what the apostle Paul wrote in 2 Corinthians 10:4-5:

> For the weapons of our warfare [are] not carnal but mighty in God for pulling down strongholds, casting down arguments and every high thing that exalts itself against the knowledge of God, bringing every thought into captivity to the obedience of Christ.

To whatever degree a sphere is operating consistent with biblical principles or, to put it another way, kingdom principles, then the kingdom of God is being manifested.

In what amounts to a dualistic fashion and compartmentalized Christianity, this verse is often limited only to a discussion of matters affecting personal piety; however, the text of the verse itself is not so limited. In other words, in addition to "things" that affect personal piety, the Christian should be trying to understand how God thinks about each of these spheres and how God thinks they should operate. And based on that understanding, the Christian should try to "cast down arguments" for the functioning of a particular sphere that are unbiblical and seek to have that sphere function instead on the basis of, and consistent with, what is true about it according to the Word of God. To whatever degree a sphere is operating consistent with biblical principles or, to put it another way, kingdom principles, then the kingdom of God is being manifested.

So, from this perspective, politics and government cannot usher in the kingdom of God. It cannot because civil government is but one sphere that is to operate according to kingdom principles. While civil government, through its regulations, can affect all the other spheres, you'll recall that, within its sphere, its purpose and its abilities are limited. Remember, civil government cannot make anyone be good. As we said earlier, it cannot make a man be a devoted, loving husband to his wife. The sphere of family has to operate according to its own kingdom principles. Success within that sphere is predicated, in part, on each member of the family, individually, living consistent with kingdom principles. This thought process extends across and through each sphere.

> **Thinking politics can usher in the kingdom of God is like thinking that our medley relay team can win a race because we have a really good freestyle swimmer.**

This is why I said the kingdom of God is like the medley relay. Thinking politics can usher in the kingdom of God is like thinking that our medley relay team can win a race because we have a really good freestyle swimmer. Every swimmer must swim every aspect of his individual race well for the race to be won, and it is no different when it comes to advancing the kingdom of God. Every sphere must function well according to biblical principles, and its function depends on each believer who is "swimming" in that sphere mastering all aspects of his particular "stroke."

However, there are those who say politics cannot usher in the kingdom of God because they believe the kingdom of God is some other-worldly phenomenon irrelevant to everyday life in the here and now. And for some, this other-worldly view of the kingdom of God justifies their disregard of politics and civil government. If that is what they mean when they say politics is limited relative to the advance of God's kingdom, then I disagree with them strongly.

Here we have expressed what some call the "battle of worldviews." As my friend, John Stonestreet, often says, "A worldview is a view of the world, for the world." In other words, a worldview is how we see the world, but it's not just a philosophic exercise. It tells us how to live in that world.

There are worldviews that are contrary to the knowledge of God. Clearly this includes those worldviews that deny God's existence. But it can also include worldviews based on belief that God exists.

> ...even if we believe God exists, we can still live like atheists

That is because even if we believe God exists, we can still live like atheists when it comes to how we view our interaction with the world. A biblical worldview, however, is one that is defined by our understanding of who God is as revealed in the Bible, and our actions should be consistent with that understanding. If we as Christians really seek to know God in truth, we will take that understanding and interpret everything else in light of it.[87] If you and I are doing this, then whatever else we may want to say about theocracy, theonomy or the kingdom of God beyond what has been said above, we are swimming the same race.

Chapter 13

Getting Over the "Wall"

—ɯ—

Some in the church might say, "What you just said seems to make sense biblically, but we live under a constitution that separates church and state." The implication, of course, is that we can't give heed to or allow the kind of thinking I've described to seep into our political thinking, presumably for legal reasons.[88]

If you are a Christian and just said that, then imagine you are standing before God Almighty, and he asks you how you stewarded the governmental authority he entrusted to you. What are you going to want to say? Now to me, *that* is a haunting question. Are you really going to reverse the words of the apostle Peter to the Council when he was brought before it for not following its command to stop preaching: We thought we ought to obey men rather than God?[89]

The non-Christian, however, cares nothing about what God says concerning stewardship or loving him. They have a completely different view of religion and Christianity in particular. In 2011, the Center for American Progress issued a report on how the homo-sexual political agenda had advanced in Tennessee. While the report spoke to what was going on in Tennessee, the statement it made regarding whether religiously informed values could be carried into the political arena applies in every state:

> While it is crucial to support the First Amendment rights of faith communities to voice their beliefs, it is also crucial to oppose their efforts to impose their theology on a pluralistic democracy.

In other words, we can speak like Christians so long as we don't try to act on those beliefs relative to political issues.

> **Practical atheism is what the world increasingly expects from Christians relative to our engagement on matters of public policy.**

Practical atheism is what the world increasingly expects from Christians relative to our engagement on matters of public policy. Absent a return to a biblical worldview, I believe more and more people will come right out and say that if the motivation for supporting a law is grounded in religiously informed values, then the law is unconstitutional.

So it is imperative that Christians have some understanding of the history of the First Amendment's provisions regarding religion and the phrase, "separation of church and state." Lots of great books have been written on this subject that have gone far deeper into it than can be done here. But here is a primer that may be of help if you don't have time to read those other books.

The first thing we need to appreciate is that all views are inherently religious. Consider this possible conversation:

> Inquisitor: You shouldn't bring your religion into politics; religion has no place in politics. It violates the separation of church and state.

Defender: I see. So you're saying that my views about God and what he says about things are "out of bounds" in public debates. And that such views violate the separation of church and state?

Inquisitor: Yes. Exactly.

Defender: Well, help me understand. My understanding of God is that he cares about what civil government does and He has established some guiding principles that are relevant to politics and political issues. Your view of God is that he's irrelevant because he doesn't exist or either he doesn't care about what government does or he doesn't have anything relevant to say about politics.

So why is your view about God relative to politics — your religious view — constitutional and mine is not? Seems like we both have a view about God and God's relationship to politics and government. Your view is as fundamentally religious as mine. The real problem is that you just don't like my view of God. So I think it would be more fruitful if we discussed the merits of our respective positions rather than which perspective about God is constitutional and which one is not.

In his *Lectures on Calvinism*, theologian and former prime minister of the Netherlands, Abraham Kuyper, put it this way, "If you exclude from your conceptions all reckoning with the Living God just as is implied in the cry, 'no God no master,' you certainly bring to the front a sharply defined interpretation of your own for our relation to God." The fact is we cannot escape having some view about God any more than we can escape making truth claims. A view about God is a religious view. God just won't allow us to ignore him.

Now let's turn to the history of the phrase "separation of church and state." While there are a number of historical considerations,

So why is your view about God relative to politics—your religious view—constitutional and mine is not?

here are a few of the key ones a Christian should know relative to Thomas Jefferson's involvement with the amendment itself.

First, the phrase does not appear anywhere in the Constitution. In fact, even the words "separation" and "church" are nowhere to be found in the Constitution. Even the singular word, "state," as opposed to the plural, "states," is nowhere to be found in the constitution. The phrase "separation of church and state" is found in a letter then President Thomas Jefferson penned to the Danbury Baptist Association in Connecticut on January 1, 1802. We'll get to the letter later.

Second, Thomas Jefferson was not even one of the 90 founding fathers at the meetings in which the U.S. Constitution was framed. Whatever Jefferson might have thought about the relationship between church and state, he wasn't there to express it or debate it.

Third, and perhaps not too surprisingly in view of the preceding fact, there is not one mention of the phrase "separation of church and state" in the *Congressional Record* of the meetings during which the 90 men who were there drafted, discussed and debated the First Amendment.

Another important historical consideration is what had been going on at a national level leading up to Jefferson's election. Prior to the election there had been growing concerns that the Federalist Party was moving toward a national government that would abandon the principles of federalism. Jefferson had just been elected president in March 1801, after a very bitter campaign in which the Federalist Party had opposed him. The Federalist Party, contrary to what the name might imply about the importance of federalism vis-a-vis states' rights, was an advocate for a strong national government. Jefferson, on the other hand, was very much a supporter of the sovereignty of the several states and a limited federal government.

The tension over states' rights versus nationalism was magnified by the fact that there had been talk among some about the possibility of establishing a national religion. A letter from Jefferson (one the U.S. Supreme Court ignored by the way) to another founding father and signer of the Declaration of Independence, Benjamin Rush, illuminates the situation.

Jefferson wrote the letter about a year before he wrote his letter to the Danbury Baptist Association and a few months prior to his election as president. It reflects how his presidency would view the First Amendment. It addresses his sentiments regarding a national ecclesiastical establishment. Keep in mind as you read it that the Danbury Baptists were under the thumb of the Congregational Church, the state church in Connecticut.

> "The clause of the Constitution which...covered...the freedom of religion, had given to the clergy a very favorite **hope of obtaining an establishment of a *particular form of Christianity* through the United States**...especially the Episcopalians **and Congregationalists**. The returning good sense of our country threatens abortion to their hopes and **they believe that any portion of power confided to me will be exerted in opposition to their schemes.** And they believe rightly. (emphasis added)

With that as background, we need to look at the Danbury letter to see what it was that Jefferson was responding to. Here are the pertinent parts of that letter:

> Our Sentiments are uniformly on the side of Religious Liberty — That Religion is at all times and places a matter

between God and individuals...But Sir our constitution of government is not specific. Our ancient charter together with the Laws made coincident therewith...considered [religion] as the first object of Legislation; and therefore *what religious privileges we enjoy (**as a minor part of the State**) we enjoy as favors granted, and not as inalienable rights*: and these favors we receive at the expense of such degrading acknowledgements, as are inconsistent with the rights of freemen. (emphasis added)

Two major issues were percolating here. One was purely political, motivated by concerns Jefferson mentioned in his letter to Benjamin Rush. The Baptists were concerned that if the federal government established some particular form of Christianity they would become a "minor part" of the nation, even as they were a "minor part" of Connecticut. In other words, they didn't want to find themselves on the proverbial outside looking in at the national level as well as at the state level. The other concern was whether Jefferson saw the right of religious liberty as a favor granted by civil government that it could control and regulate or as an inalienable right not subject to control by the civil government. Sadly, that concern is rising again in our day as Christian business owners come increasingly under attack by civil government.

At the time some saw in the enumeration of a right to free exercise of religion the implication that government was "granting" a right to free exercise and not simply acknowledging a God-given, inalienable right to free exercise, the protection of which the government should guarantee. The Baptists wanted to make sure that Jefferson would approach any efforts to establish a national church or national position on doctrinal issues as a substantive wrong, not just a procedural or constitutional wrong.

With that as background, we are ready to look at what Jefferson wrote to the Baptists:

> Believing with you that religion is a matter which lies solely between man and his God, that he owes account to none other for faith or his worship, that the legislative powers of government reach **actions only, and not opinions**, I contemplate with sovereign reverence that **act of the whole American people** which declared that **their legislature** should "make no law respecting an establishment of religion, or prohibiting the free exercise thereof" thus building a wall of separation between church and state. (emphasis added)

Breaking the letter down, we see two things. First, Jefferson was addressing specifically his views on the First Amendment relative to the powers of the federal government over religion.[90] We know this because the U.S. Constitution could be the only "act of the whole American people" relative to religion to which he could have been referring in his letter. The Baptists were not asking Jefferson to do anything about the state-church issues in Connecticut.

Second, Jefferson drew a clear distinction between laws regulating conduct and those regulating opinion. In the context of the concern then percolating in American politics about whether "a particular form of Christianity," namely, that espoused by the Episcopalians or Congregationalists, would be established "through the United States," the opinions to which he was referring were those related to theological or doctrinal issues.

In other words, Jefferson was telling the Baptists that no national *ecclesiastical authority* would be established on his watch. Jefferson didn't want any civil government dictating to him what his religious doctrinal beliefs and religious practices should be. He essentially wanted to avoid a situation like that in England where the king was the head of the church.

These are the two issues clearly touched on in Jefferson's letter. Nothing in the letter said or implied anything about how civil government should determine what actions — civil conduct — should be addressed by its policies and laws. He said nothing about whether religiously informed values could be used to determine what *civil conduct* should be encouraged or restrained by civil government. In other words, unlike what today's separationists want Americans to believe, Jefferson never indicated that he thought the policies of civil government regulating civil conduct should be separated from religiously informed values about that conduct. That wasn't the issue.

In fact, consistent with this interpretation are these other statements by Jefferson. In the Declaration of Independence he grounded the values and principles justifying our separation from England on the "Laws of nature and of nature's God."[91] He also said, "Can the liberties of a nation be thought secure, when we have removed their only firm basis, a conviction in the minds of the people that these liberties are the gift of God?"[92] In neither statement do we see Jefferson separating religious beliefs from public policy.

We must also not forget Jefferson's actions. Jefferson attended religious services held on government property. He helped developing congregations by allowing them to hold services in the Treasury and War office buildings. He signed a federal law providing a tax exemption for churches in the District of Columbia. And in 1779, as governor of Virginia[93], he appointed "a day of publick (sic) and solemn thanksgiving and prayer to Almighty God."

But let's test this construction and interpretation of the First Amendment a bit further by looking at one last person, Joseph Story, a noteworthy figure when it comes to what the U.S. Constitution, when adopted, was supposed to mean.

Mr. Story served on the United States Supreme Court for more than 30 years, from 1811 until 1845, and holds the distinction of being the youngest person ever to be appointed to the Supreme Court. He also served as Dane Professor of Law at Harvard during his time on the court. He was 10 years old at the time the U.S. Constitution went into effect so he should have been well acquainted with the history of the constitutional period. And, as a matter of fact, in 1833, he wrote the *first* comprehensive treatise on the U.S. Constitution, the three volume *Commentaries on the Constitution of the United States; with a preliminary review of the constitutional history of the colonies and states, before the adoption of the constitution.*

Here is what Justice Story wrote regarding the First Amendment:

> The real object of the First Amendment was not to countenance, much less to advance Mohammedanism, or Judaism, or infidelity, by prostrating Christianity, but to exclude **all rivalry among Christian sects** and to prevent any **national ecclesiastical establishment** which should give to an hierarchy the exclusive patronage of the national government." (emphasis added)

The concern about ecclesiastical establishment, mentioned by Justice Story is exactly the concern Jefferson was addressing in his famed letter. But Justice Story's comment deserves a closer look. What did he mean by "infidelity?" To accurately understand that word and what he meant, we need to know what the word meant at the time the statement was written, not what we may take it to mean today. Therefore, using the 1828 Noah Webster dictionary, we find that "infidelity" meant:

> 1. In general, want of faith or belief; a withholding of credit. Disbelief of the inspiration of the Scriptures, or the divine origin of Christianity; unbelief.

Thus Justice Story was saying that the First Amendment was not to be used to encourage, advance or defend atheism, a lack of belief in

God. And, at the time, the infidelity or lack of faith would have been toward Christianity. And, according to Justice Story's commentary, atheism was certainly not to be encouraged by "prostrating Christianity," which according to the 1828 Webster's dictionary, would have meant to throw down or overthrow or ruin Christianity!

In fact, when the First Amendment was written, it was not the intent at all to protect atheists from exposure to religion, as the Establishment Clause is now used. In Noah Webster's 1828 dictionary, here is how "religion" is defined:

> Religion, in its most comprehensive sense, includes a belief in the being and perfections of God, in the revelation of his will to man, in man's obligation to obey his commands, in a state of reward and punishment, and in man's accountableness to God…**the practice of moral duties without a belief in a divine lawgiver, and without reference to his will or commands, is not religion.** (emphasis added)

…it can be fairly said an atheist's rights to be free of religion was not encompassed under the First Amendment.

Atheism was *not* considered a religion and between what Justice Story said and the very definition of the word "religion" in the First Amendment, it can be fairly said an atheist's rights to be free of religion was not encompassed under the First Amendment. And for sure, as we said previously, the First Amendment was not to be used to encourage, advance or defend atheism by tearing Christianity down.

The bottom line: *the First Amendment is being used today to do exactly the opposite of what Justice Story said. It is being used to advance atheism by prostrating Christianity!*

Have we interpreted Justice Story correctly? Well, here is how he prefaced the earlier statement we analyzed:

> Probably at the time of the adoption of the constitution, and of the amendment to it, now under consideration, the general, if not the universal, sentiment in America was, that **Christianity ought to receive encouragement from the state,** so far as was not incompatible with the private rights of conscience, and the freedom of religious worship. An attempt to level all religions, and **to make it a matter of state policy to hold all in utter indifference, would have created universal disapprobation, if not universal indignation.** (emphasis added)

So what was the First Amendment supposed to do? It was to keep the institutional jurisdiction of the church—again, as an institution—separate from the institutional jurisdiction of the civil government. And it was to protect the church from intrusion by the civil government.

The bottom line: *the First Amendment is being used today to do exactly the opposite of what Justice Story said. It is being used to advance atheism by prostrating Christianity!*

All that does not mean that voters either must or cannot take into account a candidate's religious beliefs or lack thereof. Under the U.S. Constitution religious belief does not qualify a person to run for office nor does the lack of belief disqualify a person. But any attempt to hold public policies regulating civil conduct unconstitutional because the policy was informed by moral values grounded in religious beliefs would stand the First Amendment on its head.

To turn a political phrase made famous in another context, it's time to tell the Supreme Court to "tear down that wall."

Conclusion

—〽—

We end where we began, with the statement by Martin Luther: "Where the battle rages, there the loyalty of the soldier is proved, and to be steady on all the battlefront beside, is but mere flight and disgrace if he flinches as that point."

If what he said is true, then when it comes to the matter of politics, where the battle certainly rages, "flight" and "disgrace" may well be words Luther would use to describe the evangelical church's attitude and many of those who fill its pews and pulpits.

When we see that we can, and indeed must, be engaged in politics in a way that fulfills the two greatest commandments—to love God and to love our neighbor—then all pretense for not being engaged is stripped away. We are confronted with what can be described as nothing less than a lack of absolute trust in the sovereign rule of God and the sufficiency of

> **We are confronted with what can be described as nothing less than a lack of absolute trust in the sovereign rule of God and the sufficiency of the grace of Christ to sustain us in whatever ills may come our way from having engaged.**

the grace of Christ to sustain us in whatever ills may come our way from having engaged. And when we get to the root of that, it can be seen as nothing other than rebellion against the authority of God over our lives.

That is a hard statement to make and hard to hear. It was hard for me. In other words, I am not just talking to others, but also to myself. The full reality of what has been said in all the preceding chapters, that I have believed for years, did not come home to me with such full force until I read Watchman Nee's book, *Spiritual Authority*. At the very beginning of his book, he makes this statement:

"The controversy of the universe is who shall have authority."

When I read that, one aspect of the overarching story of Scripture became clearer to me than ever before. It is the story of God's response to Adam's rebellion against his authority by which all of us descending from Adam were eternally separated from him. Scripture, therefore, is the story of God bringing forth a "second Adam" in the person of Jesus to re-establish the principle of obedience in man rightly realigned under God's authority.

And it is the opportunity, through faith in Jesus and his life in us, for us not only to be justified again before God, bringing us back into an eternal relationship with him, but also to have the power through faith to live with fidelity under God's lawful authority. That is a mouthful, but the issue of authority gave a whole new meaning to me of why the author of Hebrews wrote that Jesus, "*even though a Son*," had to "learn obedience."[94] (emphasis added)

Then pastor Nee wrote something else that I think Christians in America, concerned about our nation's downward trajectory, need to hear:

"Nothing will be solved until the issue of authority is resolved."

That is the point of this book. It is the bottom line when it comes to whether and how we Christians will engage in politics.

The issues facing America will not be resolved because of the economic philosophy we follow, the tax policies we implement, the strategies we adopt relative to foreign nations, and other such things. Those things are important and getting them "right" as understood in light of God's principles is better than getting them wrong; however, *the real issue facing America is whether the Body of Christ, and more specifically you and I, will repent of our rebellion against God's authority in relationship to the tangible manifestation of it that we call civil government.*

> *...the real issue facing America is whether the Body of Christ, and more specifically you and I, will repent of our rebellion against God's authority in relationship to the tangible manifestation of it that we call civil government.*

More specifically, the question is whether we will repent of the rebellion demonstrated in our failure to steward well, according to God's precepts and principles, the authority God entrusted to us in our form of government. Will we recognize again that for a Christian to run for elected office is a high calling to ministry, to service as a "diakonos"[95] of God, and repent of seeing it as some secular pursuit less important than singing in the choir or teaching a Sunday school class? Will we repent of allowing our vote to be blindly given in allegiance to some political party or other establishment of man, and offer it back to God in allegiance only to him?

To me, at least, recovering our understanding of the rightful authority of God over all things and our submission to him in all things, regardless of the temporal cost, is nothing less than another Great Awakening[96] and a particular aspect of that awakening in relationship to politics. Charles Finney, a budding lawyer turned evangelist, was a leader in the Second Great Awakening. Thus it is fitting that we conclude our thoughts on the subject of politics with a statement he made that is every bit as true now as it was then:

> The Church must take *right ground* to politics...The time has come for Christians to vote for honest men, and take consistent ground in politics or the Lord will curse them... God cannot sustain this free and blessed country, which we love and pray for, *unless the church will take right ground.* Politics are a part of religion in such a country as this, and Christians must do this duty to their country *as part of their duty to God*...God will bless or curse this nation according to the course Christians take in politics."[97] (emphasis added)

Finney's words ring as true today as they did then. This time we should heed them, and I would submit that at least part of that "right ground" is seeing engagement in politics as:

an act of obedience to God

by which we express

our love for him and

our love for our neighbor

through the faithful stewardship of the civil authority he has entrusted to us.

Now the question is what will you and I do with the knowledge we have gained? How will we steward it? Will our love for God and for our neighbor be such that if God comes looking for us tomorrow he will find us engaged where the battle of our day rages? I pray it is so![98]

Appendix

—∭—

In Chapter 10, we looked at the issue of rights, arguing that for there to be any real rights that government *should* respect and protect, they must come from our Creator. And to that end, the case was made that, at least for the Christian, those rights were to be found and should be grounded in the Ten Commandments. Certain basic principles were then drawn from those premises. However, there is value in looking at how these principles might be applied in "real life" situations.

Let us begin that process of application by starting with an easy situation: should there be a law against murder? To my knowledge everyone agrees that taking an *innocent* life is evil.[99] But the question for the Christian, using the above principles, is, "Why is that evil?" For something to be evil it must, by definition, violate some real and true good. The good in this case is the attack on and destruction of the image of God in man. Thus, we have the sixth commandment prohibiting murder and the positive right to life that the prohibition protects. It is for that primary reason, not for utilitarian purposes or practical reasons, a Christian opposes murder.

So, by punishing murder, civil government can punish and hopefully restrain an evil and, in doing so, encourage respect for life.[100] In addition, a law punishing murder does not violate another person's positive rights. For example, a law prohibiting murder does not violate the positive right to life of any person outside that of the murderer. The murderer, having no right to do wrong, has forfeited his positive right for the sake of justice. By restraining the evil of violating a person's positive right to life and by not violating the positive rights of any other person in the process, the law is being used lawfully. Substantively, it is lawful because it treats as evil what is evil. Likewise, as a matter of procedure, the law is being used lawfully because it is directed at a wrongdoer without restraining or punishing a good (does not do evil for the sake of doing good) and without being directed at one who does good.

Now let's go a little deeper by going back to the issue of dishonesty. Consistent with the ninth commandment, every person has a positive right to be dealt with honestly.[101] To protect that right, civil government can restrain various types of dishonest dealings by punishing them. That is simple enough. And a law punishing a dishonest practice violates no positive right of any person. Additionally, by punishing dishonesty, over time honesty may be encouraged. So laws restraining or punishing dishonesty in our dealings with one another can be good.

But can we use the law to make someone honest, to make someone "be" good? We have previously said that the law cannot make a person be or do good, and at first blush, we'd probably say "no" in this particular instance. But someone playing the role of devil's advocate might say that is not completely true. The law could authorize various means of torture so severe that it would "make" a person tell the truth. Now while telling the truth under duress does not make one honest, as a matter of righteousness, a "sufficient" level of duress could produce an honest answer to whatever is in question. So why do we tend to recoil at the thought of laws that authorize torture?

Here would be a good place to introduce the notion of what I call derivative rights. Derivative rights, as I use the term, are rights that can be derived from the existence of one of the positive rights protected by the Ten Commandments. We recognize these kinds of rights all the time. For example, if by the eighth (do not steal) and sixth (do not murder) commandments, respectively, I have a positive right to possess my property and my own person, then I should also have a right to freedom of speech and association and should not be compelled to be a witness against myself. As with my positive rights, the civil government should protect these derivative rights so long as doing so does not violate or restrain another person's positive or derivative rights. And not surprisingly, our founding fathers, operating from a biblical worldview, protected these rights in our Bill of Rights. They didn't pluck these rights out of thin air; there was a basis for them.

> **...our founding fathers, operating from a biblical worldview, protected these rights in our Bill of Rights. They didn't pluck these rights out of thin air; there was a basis for them.**

But before proceeding further, it would be good to state explicitly what has been said implicitly. Implicit in this discussion of positive and derivative rights is that individual rights are limited to those rights and values (and those derived from them) that are protected in the Ten Commandments. Thus, there is no right to health care, though there is a right to have my body protected from harm. There is no right to a certain level of income, though there is a right to own and possess property by lawful means (i.e., not by stealing).

While this limitation would infuriate many in politics today, it is consistent with the belief of our founders that real rights are those that are inalienable and that those rights can only come from our Creator. As our modern culture has disavowed the existence or relevance of a Creator, we have created (no pun intended) a situation in which there is no societal basis for saying what is or is not a right. It seems that "rights" today are determined by the power possessed by the person or group asserting the right.

While this limitation would infuriate many in politics today, it is consistent with the belief of our founders that real rights are those that are inalienable and that those rights can only come from our Creator.

With that being said, let's go back to the example of torture. In this situation the law could not authorize torture without violating the positive rights of the person being tortured. It is an attack on the person's positive right to physical security and bodily integrity as an image bearer of God. This right flows from the prohibition on murder in the same way that the right to life does, the wrong in this situation being only one of a lesser degree than murder. Furthermore, it should be noted that the authorization of torture would violate the tortured person's derivative rights to freedom of speech and freedom from self-incrimination.[102] I suggest it is for these reasons that we generally outlaw torture. However, in doing so we do not violate the positive rights of any other person. There is no positive right to torture another person. The bottom line is that we cannot get at the truth by means of torture without violating another person's derivative rights.

Let's consider another issue related to the right to honest dealings with others that can be derived from the ninth commandment. As an image bearer of God, Person A has the positive right not to have that image marred by another's lie. At the same time, Person B, his neighbor, has a right to freedom of speech derived from their right to have the possession of their own person protected. Now suppose that Person B, upset with Person A, begins to lie about his neighbor to others in a defamatory way.[103] Applying the hypothesis under consideration, is a law against defamation a "good" law?

Based on what has been said so far, we might say, "no," because the law would seem to violate Person B's derivative right to free speech. However, here we find a subtle but important distinction. Person A has the positive right not to be defamed, derived from the ninth commandment's prohibition on bearing false testimony. So, while Person B has the right to freedom of speech, he does not have the right to do wrong; namely, to defame his neighbor, defamation being a form of lying prohibited by the ninth commandment.

But still, we might ask, doesn't a law punishing defamation violate Person B's positive rights to freedom of speech? No, because Person B still has the right to speak to others about his neighbor. Person B just can't lie to them about his neighbor. As previously stated, there is no right to do wrong and to lie is wrong. Positive rights are circumscribed by the principle that one cannot exercise them in ways that are wrong or do evil, violating another's positive rights. And it also should be noted that restraining Person B from lying does not violate any other positive right Person B has.

But now let's dig even a little deeper and make the issue even a bit more complicated. We have said that murder is an attack on the image of God. In fact, we might say it is the ultimate attack upon the image of God in man. But what about other acts that deny, mar or disrespect the image of God in man such as being a "respecter of persons"[104] based upon a person's race, sex or economic status. We see conduct that discriminates on the basis of sex, ethnicity/race, and economic status condemned in Scripture.[105] Having the right to be free of such discrimination could be seen as a right derived from the image of God in man to be protected by the commandment against murder. So what about a law that punishes another person for discriminating? Is that a good law?

Consider this scenario. A person owns an apartment. It is his property. But the owner is a respecter of persons and will not allow a person of a certain ethnicity to rent from him. To restrain this evil, civil government passes a law that forbids "discrimination in housing." The law certainly has restrained an evil, but has the law been used lawfully? Does the law violate some positive right of another person, in this case the positive rights of the person owning the rental property? To analyze this question, we have to consider what is here involved from the perspective of both the prospective tenant and property owner.

Looking at the situation relative to the property owner first, his position in one way is no different from that of the lying neighbor in the preceding example. The lying neighbor had no positive right to lie, and the property owner has no positive right to do wrong, namely, to discriminate.

But unlike the lying neighbor, the owner of property does has a positive right, consistent with the eighth commandment, to own property without it being taken and given to another.[106] Having the positive right to own property entails the right to *possess* and to *dispose* of one's property. Interference in the full rights associated with one's ownership of his or her property is a violation of that person's positive rights.[107]

Consequently, in this situation, if the civil government passes a law that requires the property owner to rent his property to anyone who is willing to pay for it at the time it is made available on the market, then the law is violating the owner's positive right to property ownership. It has violated the owner's right to dispose of his property, a right derived from the positive right to own property.[108]

While this thought is probably a jolt to our modern way of thinking, it must be kept in mind that this is an entirely different situation from those in which the civil government itself is perpetrating the act of wrongful discrimination. The conduct of private actors in their private relationships with one another is fundamentally different from that of civil government's actions against its own citizens. Consider the distinction, earlier made, regarding individuals versus the magistrate as it related to who God allows to express God's vengeance and wrath against evil. This understanding is also in keeping with the original understanding of our Bill of Rights. The Bill of Rights served as a limitation on civil government relative to citizens, not as a limitation on the private conduct of citizens toward one another.

But what about the rights of the person wanting to rent or buy the property? While the prospective renter has a positive right not to be discriminated against, he does not have a positive right to interfere with another person's possession and ownership of his property. This would be the right to do wrong in order to achieve the good of being able to own property. Nor does the potential renter have a right to live on any particular piece of property. The potential renter does have a right to his own property, but not a right to another's property.

Note, however, that this is not a case in which the law denies the renter the right to own or rent property at all. A law denying a person the right to own or rent property at all would necessarily violate the person's affirmative right to own property. That right is derived from the positive right to be protected from theft found in the eighth commandment's prohibition against stealing. Furthermore, a law denying a person the right to own any property violates the positive right of a property owner to dispose of his property to that person. But the renter cannot be given the right to own or possess any specific property without violating the positive right of property in the person owning it.

> **...this seems like an anathema to modern ears, but this is so only because we have not understood our own constitution.**

Again, this seems like an anathema to modern ears, but this is so only because we have not understood our own constitution. As previously stated, the Bill of Rights protects the individual from actions by the civil government and does not touch private interactions. Because of that, some property owners found a way to impose their discriminatory attitudes toward African-Americans on others when it came to selling their property by restricting the right of their purchasers to resell the property to African-Americans. These were called deed restrictions.

Eventually the injustice of these deed restrictions reached the U.S. Supreme Court. The Court rightly wanted to stop such actions. But it was faced with the fact that this was a private transaction; the civil government had not created the deed restriction. Therefore, the Court had to find a way to ascribe some kind of "state action" to a private act of the seller in order to "step in." The Court found a way to accomplish this on the ground that these deed restrictions could not be enforced between a willing buyer and willing seller without the "state action" of a court enforcing the deed restriction.[109]

In trying to do the "right thing," the door was opened to people suing to stop some private action they didn't like on the ground that there was some "state action" involved, even though indirect or remote. There is now a whole line of cases trying to establish the "criteria" by which state action will be attributed to a private person. Such deed restrictions should have been made unlawful legislatively by statute as a restriction on the ownership of property.[110]

But laying aside the preceding, complicated constitutional analysis, let's look at it this way. If you and I were personally to interfere with or take away another's right to dispose of his property, we would call it stealing. So is the *nature* of the act any different when the taking is done pursuant to a housing law passed by civil government? In other words, can the government steal? God thinks so, and He condemns it. The condemnation heaped upon King Ahab for killing Naboth, who was without heirs, in order to subsequently seize his land makes it clear that God thinks the civil government, by means of the law, can steal.[111] This story is an example of what was said earlier about the statement in 1 Timothy 3:9 that the law can be used unlawfully.

However, part of the reason that the law cannot "fix" the problem of wrongful private discrimination[112] is that it is really an attitude of the heart. And while attitudes can break out into action,[113] the law has a hard time judging the heart.[114] In the previous example, the property owner may not have rented to the individual, not because of the person's ethnicity, but because his sloppy appearance made the landlord think the person would not care for the property properly. Maybe the property owner didn't rent the property because an attitude was perceived during the showing of the property that made him believe that the person might be an unsuitable neighbor for existing fellow tenants.

In such situations, it would be easy enough for the person looking for a place to rent to assume he was denied a lease because of his ethnicity and to sue. But even as we can have a hard time discerning the motives of our own heart, let alone that of others, the law can have a hard time discerning the truth of the situation involving the rental property and the landowner's heart. Furthermore, apart from making discriminatory statements outright, the good intent of the law is easily frustrated by a careful owner coming up with some non-discriminatory reason for not renting the property.

Before closing this chapter, though, it would be good to consider one last situation in which we might try to punish a wrong attitude of the heart and "encourage" others to do good or the "right thing," namely, to punish or restrain the "wrong" of greed and to promote or encourage the "good" of charity toward those who are less fortunate than ourselves. In today's politics, there is much talk of economic disparities, fairness, greed and the rich versus the poor.

The noble goal of reducing greed and encouraging charity is most often done through civil government's welfare programs and a plan of taxation that redistributes some amount of property from those who have a certain level of income to those who do not have an amount that civil government has determined is a minimal amount.[115] Perhaps those who support such policies feel that they are accomplishing something good. They may think they are helping the poor by providing them resources. And they may think that they are punishing evil through the taxation of those whose greed has caused them to hoard their property to the detriment of the poor.

The good the civil government is trying to do with the law in this instance, when we boil it all down, is to do the good of helping people by trying either to make some people be more "charitable" or make others less greedy. But, when we put it that way, we recoil because we know that we can't make people be charitable. If a person's giving isn't a free, volitional act, then, by definition, it is not charitable (and taxes do not represent a giving, but a taking in any event). And by taking from someone the property he has greedily hoarded to himself, we don't make him less greedy; he just has less. Greed, like charity, is also a matter of the heart.

Interestingly, with respect to the intersection of law and issues of the heart, Scripture gives us a case in point. Luke 12 recounts the story of a young man who came to Jesus, saying, "Teacher, tell my brother to divide the inheritance with me." Apparently the young man did not like the inheritance laws because, in his opinion, the law allowed his brother to be greedy. The brother apparently took all the inheritance that the law allowed and rebuffed his brother's request for a "fairer" share of it.

But Jesus did not say or even indicate that the law needed to be adjusted to restrain the brother's greed, as perceived by the young man, or to create a more equitable outcome. Rather Jesus essentially responded that he was not the probate judge, and then turned the tables on the young man by telling him to watch out for the greed, lurking in his own heart, that had been revealed by his complaint against his brother. The bottom line is that this was an attitude of the heart that only Jesus, not the "probate" laws, could rightly deal with.

In response to the story in Luke, some might say that it is all right that the law can't make greedy people generous because the law is still being used to help the poor and that is good by anyone's definition.[116] But let's not go there quite so fast. Leaving aside the question whether civil government welfare programs actually help the poor long term,[117] we run into the other problem we have previously discussed; namely, that the law is being used to violate a positive right. But in this case, the law is not even protecting a right in the person trying to be helped.

While a poor person has the positive right to earn property and to the secure possession of the property so earned, we never find in Scripture any indication that there is a positive right to any certain amount of property.[118] So a "welfare" law is not vindicating any positive right of any person, but it is violating the positive right to property of the person from whom the money is being taken. To justify government theft because the end—helping the poor or punishing greed—is good is to ignore the principle that the ends cannot be used to justify unlawful means, which we previously noted is condemned by the passage in First Timothy.

...we should always be careful not to presume that a result reached through the use of unaided reason is better than one produced by a careful, discerning and reasoned application of biblical principles.

There may be situations in which the analysis in this chapter produces a result with which we may not feel comfortable. Yet, as Christians we should always be careful not to presume that a result reached through the use of unaided reason is better than one produced by a careful, discerning and reasoned application of biblical principles. Even then, however, humility bids us all to consider that others may have insights that can improve upon or refine our own analysis of Scripture.

But unless our analysis as Christians is grounded in an attempt to apply the truth of the Word of God, we will have no foundation upon which to build our laws or to reason together. And we will have to join the late Professor Leff in concluding that there is no final solution to our recognized need to ground our rights and our laws on something more than human will measured by votes, money or guns. However difficult the struggle might be to analyze and grapple with biblical principles in order to apply them, and however uncomfortable we may become with our conclusions based on those principles, God's Word says the results will be worth the effort and God's claim to our obedience deserves nothing less.

Discussion Questions and Study Guide

—ʍ—

Introduction:

<u>Discussion Questions:</u>

1. What were your thoughts as you read the statement by Martin Luther in the introduction?

2. Have you ever been around people with impressive credentials or who were well known in your community? How did you feel around them? What do you think made you feel that way?

3. Do you think the people you know, particularly Christians, have made an "idol" out of politics? If so, what are some of the things that led you to that conclusion?

4. Where are some of the "raging battles" being fought in your own life at which you are most tempted to "flinch." Have everyone pray for each other about those "battles" during the course of your study together.

For Further Study:

First Corinthians 1:25-29. What do these verses tell us about how God views those qualities that the world looks at as being valuable or distinguishing?

Acts 4:13. What does it seem the people would have expected to be true about Peter and John in view of the confidence they exhibited? What did the people realize was true about them? What can we learn from these verses about what should or should not influence our evaluation of others and what they have to say?

Chapter 1: The Politics of Hate

Discussion Questions:

1. What are some of your general attitudes toward politics and politicians?

2. Have you ever been in a situation or a relationship in which you knew you were called to love a person, but their wrong choices made loving them hard? What do you think made it hard?

3. Why do you think so many people today think of Christians as hateful and intolerant when it comes to their views on political issues or their involvement in politics?

4. Has the attitude of others towards Christians and politics affected your willingness to share your views on an issue or get involved in politics? If so, in what ways?

For Further Study:

Mark 3:22-27; Luke 11:15-22. How does this story relate to the "name calling" of the politics of hate? How did Jesus handle it?

First Peter 2:12. What can we learn from this verse about what others may say about us if we seek to live godly lives? In what ways does this verse challenge you going forward?

Chapter 2: Maybe Hate Isn't So Bad After All

Discussion Questions:

1. What statement or promise in Scripture do you most often struggle to believe to the point of acting on it?

2. Have you ever had anyone hate you or stop wanting to be around you because you were trying to live out, by words or actions, your faith in Christ? What were your thoughts and feelings about it at the time and what impact or influence did it have on you going forward?

3. How do you think the world defines being hateful? How does that definition compare to how you think God would define it? Do you think non-Christians today, if they read some of what Jesus said to the Scribes, Pharisees and Sadducees would say Jesus was hateful? If so, do any particular verses come to mind in that regard?

4. What about your beliefs would have to change in order for you to be more willing than you are now to share your views on issues with others or become more engaged with the political process?

For Further Study:

Jeremiah 20:7-11. Have you ever felt like Jeremiah relative to how others perceive you as a Christian? If not, have you ever been concerned that you would be treated like Jeremiah if your Christianity were too obvious at work, school, or in other non-Christian social settings? If so, in what way did those concerns affect what you said or did?

Matthew 10:34-37; James 4:3-4. Can a Christian or the Church be true to the gospel of Jesus Christ and expect to avoid conflict and division with those who are not Christians? Why or why not? What verses support your conclusion?

Chapter 3: Power Politics

Discussion Questions:

1. Are you or have you ever been in a position of power or authority over some situation, decision, or person that, for you, was significant? What were your thoughts and feelings at that time both about yourself and those who might be affected by how you used that authority?

2. Prior to reading this Chapter, had you ever thought about where civil government's power comes from? If not, why do you think that is the case? If you had, what were your thoughts and did those thoughts affect the way you voted or what position you took on a political issue? If so, in what ways?

3. How do you think most Christian and non-Christians would react to the proposition that the power they hold as voters and the power their elected officials hold comes from God and that they will be accountable to God for how they use it?

4. If the true source of civil government's power is found in God, why do you think the leadership of a local church would refuse to talk about what God's Word says regarding current political and governmental issues?

For Further Study:

Psalm 14:1. What is God's judgment regarding those who would deny his existence? Can you think of things people do, say, or believe that are hard to explain or justify if there is no God?

Proverbs 16:10. What makes the judgment of those who make law "divine?" As you consider the implications of this verse, what thoughts come to your mind about those you authorize by your vote to make laws on your behalf?

Chapter 4: Loving God

Discussion Questions:

1. Have you ever had a special relationship with someone who was not a member of your family? What made it special?

2. What crossed your mind when you read the statement, "Christians *can* engage in politics without being hateful *if* our purpose and focus are defined in terms of God?"

3. How do you think non-Christians think of Christian involvement in politics and why?

4. If engaging in our political system is an issue of stewardship, how would you evaluate your stewardship and what specific things would you need to do to better steward the authority you hold in our form of government?

For Further Study:

Matthew 25:14-19, 24-30. What do these verses teach us about stewardship and how God looks at its importance? If the "power of the ballot box" is a delegated authority from God, how do you think God would look at the fact that some Christians don't vote?

Acts 20:17-21, 26-28. What did Paul not do (verses 20, 27) that, by implication, some who teach and preach the word of God might tend to do? How does Paul's approach to the breadth of his teaching compare to the teaching you have had within the local church regarding God's purpose for civil government and politics?

Chapter 5: Getting Off Track

Discussion Questions:

1. Can you think of a time when you wound up in situation of some kind you had not anticipated? If appropriate, share it with the group and any "lesson" you came away with.

2. Can you think of an aspect of your life or thinking that God has been telling you might be "off track" in terms biblical principles or about which you have told God, "hands off?" If appropriate, share it with the group and have the group pray with you about it.

3. What do you think are the most common attitudes among non-Christians today about the relevance of Scripture to political issues and policy concerns and why? How do you think Christians have contributed to those attitudes?

4. Is there an issue in politics about which you have not given much thought in terms of Scripture and a biblical world-view? What do you plan to do to learn more about that issue?

For Further Study:

Isaiah 17-10-11. Thinking about the images portrayed in these verses, do you see any parallels to what is going on in the United States? If so, what are they?

Colossians 2:1-3, 8. What is it that keeps us from being deceived by unbiblical ideas that "get us off track?" What can you do to grow in your knowledge of the nature and character of the Triune God?

Chapter 6: Praise and Punishment

Discussion Questions:

1. Have you ever attended a political event or interacted with an elected official, whether on a political or purely personal level? What were your thoughts about that experience?

2. Because civil government "bears the sword"—has the authority to use force—what possible consequences come to your mind if that force is used to encourage that which God's Word says is evil or to restrain that which God's Word says is good?

3. What do you think are the most prevalent thoughts today about the purpose for which civil government should exercise its power? How well do you think those thoughts conform to Scripture and why?

4. Romans 5:4 says, "Those who do good have nothing to fear." Do you feel that way about your federal, state and local governments? What do you think your answer says about whether those governments are functioning biblically?

For Further Study:

Isaiah 5:20-24. As you read these verses, what thoughts come to mind relative to the statement in 1 Peter 2:14 that the ruler's actions will be associated with a judgment regarding what is good and evil?

Romans 2:14-16. In what way do these verses relate to the story with which this chapter began? Can you think of other things people do or say that show they believe something they profess to deny?

Chapter 7: Who says?

<u>Discussion Questions:</u>

1. Have you ever been in or observed a conversation in which someone would just not answer the question being asked? Share your experience and how it made you feel?

2. In the chapter it was said that many Christians "either give no consideration to God and his Word when it comes to law and government, or they only give them lip service." How would you rate yourself in that regard on a scale of 1 to 10, and why? Do you think this statement is true with respect to the majority of Christians? Why or why not?

3. Professor Leff asked who among us, in the absence of the God of the Bible, ought to be able to declare a law that everyone ought to obey. Do you think most Americans who argue for a "separation of church and state" have thought about that question? Why or why not? What do you think the most common answer would be to that question?

4. Who might be someone you could encourage to think more deeply about the source of civil government's authority and how might you do that?

<u>For Further Study:</u>

Isaiah 59:3-9, 14. What is the relationship between the kind of culture we experience and truth? Can justice and righteousness exist in a society in the absence of truth? Why or why not?

Romans 1:21, 25-26, 28-32. What happens when we cease to worship and acknowledge the Creator?

Chapter 8: Loving My Neighbor

Discussion Questions:

1. Can you think of a situation in which you or someone else didn't listen to or seek sound advice and wound up "learning the hard way?" If appropriate, share with the group what you did and what you would do differently today.

2. Consider at what level or degree you engage in political matters (talking with others about issues, evaluating candidates and those for whom you vote, voting frequency, campaign involvement, etc). On a scale of 1 to 10, how often is your primary motivation for engaging in such matters self-interest as opposed to the well-being of others or the common good?

3. What do you think are the primary reasons people do or do not get involved in politics? What do you think are some of the primary reasons people vote for a particular candidate?

4. In what practical ways do you think you could better love your neighbor when it comes to what our laws will praise or restrain?

For Further Study:

I Kings15:25-34. What do these verses say about the relationship between kings (government leaders) and the effect they can have on the people they govern?

Proverbs 19:2. What does this verse say about those who rule and their effect on the welfare of the people? What kind of person should we give our vote to if we regard the welfare of our neighbors important?

Chapter 9: Putting the Pieces Together

Discussion Questions:

1. While there may be several, what is one of your most important principles by which you try to live and why is it important to you?

2. What thoughts came to your mind as you read about the "Adamic Shift?"

3. Do you think enough thought is given to the Adamic shift and its consequences in American politics? Can you think of a law or policy that, in your opinion, effectively takes into consideration or fails to adequately take into consideration the "Adamic Shift?" Why do you think it does or does not?

4. Have you ever complained about a policy/law that civil government has enacted or failed to enact? At its root, what principle or value did you think was being violated or ignored? Can you think of some policy or law you favor that, if considered honestly, would really violate or ignore that same principle or value?

For Further Study:

Romans 7:15-25. Was Paul's problem that he didn't know what was the right thing to do? How do you think a majority of people in America and our elected officials think about education relative to the problems facing America? Do you think Paul would agree with them? Why or why not?

Ephesians 2:1-3. What do these verses teach us about the goodness of people prior to God's saving work in their lives? Do you think these verses teach that people do "good" things despite a sinful nature or that they do bad things despite an innate goodness?

Chapter 10: Lawful Laws

<u>Discussion Questions:</u>

1. Have you ever been in a situation in which someone was acting according to the "letter of the law," but violating the spirit of it to their advantage or to the disadvantage of someone else? What were your thoughts and feelings at the time? What, if anything, did you do?

2. Have you ever been in a situation in which you asserted a right or had someone assert a right against you? What right was at issue and upon what authority did you or the other person base that right?

3. Name some of the rights being asserted today? Can you identify a Scriptural ground for them? Are rights not grounded either directly or indirectly in Scripture rights that civil government is morally and ethically bound to protect? Why or why not?

4. What would you say to a person who said to you, "Well, that's the law so live with it" or something to that effect.

<u>For Further Study:</u>

Deuteronomy 4:5-6. Did God anticipate that other nations would realize the wisdom of the statutes and ordinance of Israel simply by reading them? Do you think the perspective non-Christians have of the way Christians live their lives helps or hinders our credibility in advocating for biblical principles in the public square?

Psalm 33:10-11. What does the Psalmist have to say about the relative stability of the counsel and plans devised by man versus those of the Lord? Based on the comparison what could we say about laws and policies grounded in the wisdom of men versus those rooted in the word of God? What do you think these verses have to say about the importance of those for whom we vote having a biblical worldview?

Chapter 11: The Politics of Loving God and Loving My Neighbor

Discussion Questions:

1. Have you ever been in a situation in which you felt like you had to "pick sides?" What was the choice? How did you decide which "side" to pick or otherwise wind up resolving the matter?

2. What are your most common fears and what do you think they reveal about you and your relationship to God?

3. What are the most common fears that you see among those you know? What do you think those fears reveal about them?

4. Has fear ever factored into your decision not to say something to others about a political issue you really do care about, not to attend a political function, not to sign a petition, or not to attend a public hearing What was it you feared? What would have to change for you to overcome that fear?

For Further Study:

First John 4:18-19. When fear creeps into our hearts and minds, what does that tell us about our understanding of God's love for us in those moments?

Jeremiah 38:4-6. Did what Jeremiah say "turn people off?" Do you think the reaction of others meant that Jeremiah was not doing or saying what he should? Would you say Jeremiah was being "effective?" Why or why not?

Chapter 12: Not a Theocracy, but the Kingdom of God

Discussion Questions:

1. Before reading this chapter, what might you have said to someone who asked you to explain what the word "theonomy" meant or what the Kingdom of God was?

2. We are exhorted by 2 Corinthians 10:5 to bring "every thought into captivity to the obedience of Christ." When you read this verse, what kind of thoughts, perspectives, or areas of life and culture do you usually think of as needing to be taken captive in obedience to Christ? Do you think there is a scriptural basis for limiting the verse to any particular kinds of thoughts, things about which we might have a perspective, or areas of life and culture?

3. How do you think most Christians and non-Christians would respond if you said you wanted to see the kingdom of God advance? Why do you think they would respond that way?

4. Can you think of one aspect of your life or a cultural issue that you need to examine or re-examine in light of God's word? How might you go about turning those thoughts into acts of obedience to Christ?

For Further Study:

Isaiah 9:7. What does this verse say about the relationship between God and government and the extent of his governing authority? Do you think of the verse in a way that excludes God as the foundation for civil government? If so, what verses support that conclusion?

Isaiah 30:1-3, 31:1-3; Amos 8:4-6. Were the issues of concern to God in these passages related to issues of national security and economic policies and practices, respectively, or only to issues of personal piety?

Chapter 13: Getting Over the "Wall"

<u>Discussion Questions:</u>

1. When was the last time you thought about what the religious liberty clauses of the First Amendment mean? What made you think about it at that time. What were your thoughts?

2. What were your thoughts as you read the comments by Justice Story about the First Amendment?

3. How do you think the people you know would respond if you asked them, "Can the government protect the free exercise of religion, as the First Amendment requires, and at the same time protect atheists from being exposed to any kind of outward expression of religion in public settings?"

4. What would you say to a person who objects to your view on a subject on the grounds that your view is religiously motivated?

<u>For Further Study:</u>

Psalm 2:1-12. How might these verses address the objection that God's truth and laws only apply to Christians or only to the nation of Israel?

Acts 17:30-31. After reading these verses, what do you think Paul would say to those who are concerned about Christians injecting their beliefs into a society made up of people with different belief systems?

Conclusion

<u>Discussion Questions:</u>

1. Have you ever struggled with submitting to someone in authority over you, perhaps a parent, employer, teacher, or coach? What made it hard to submit?

2. What were your thoughts when you read the statement by Charles Finney about the church's role and responsibility toward the future well being of America?

3. Have you ever watched a friend's life get complicated or unravel because he or she kept making choices contrary to God's word? What were your thoughts and feelings when you saw that happening? Did you try to intervene in some way? If so, what happened?

4. At the beginning, what were some of your reasons for reading this book and your thoughts about Christian involvement in politics? Having read the book, have any of those thoughts been reinforced, challenged, or changed? Which ones and in what way?

<u>For Further Study:</u>

Amos 5:18-24; Jeremiah 7:21-24. What do these verses teach us about obedience and religious observances?

Ephesians 1:15-23. Do you think this passage can fairly be read to exclude political and governmental power from being subject to Christ's authority in the present age? Why or why not? Do you tend to think of God as giving Christ to the church as ruler over all things or only as ruler over all things pertaining to the church? Why or why not?

Endnotes

Preface

Introduction

[1] I responded to his questions with an explanatory memo and ended it with my own question: "If you are right, in the absolute sense, that homosexuality is okay, then I must ask you further, in all sincerity and humility, on what basis do you know that truth? Please do not say logic or reason because, as indicated above, that will lead us only to our own opinions and then who, among men, is to say who is right?" I never got a reply. Interestingly, several years later, my partner came up to me in the break room and began to attack my views on something else. I held up my hand and said I was happy to discuss this with him, but not until he told me how he knew he was right. I reminded him I was still waiting for an answer to that question from several years earlier. Fascinatingly, he said, "I knew you would bring that up." He knew he had never answered my question. And I still have no answer.

[2] And for what it is worth, I taught some of what is in this book for four years at a Christian liberal arts college.

[3] Philippians 3:7-8.

[4] Second Corinthians 10:5.

Chapter 1

[5] Starnes, Todd (July 25, 2012). "Rahm: 'Chick-fil-A Values Are Not Chicago Values.'" *Fox News Radio*; Collier, Myles (July 18, 2012). "Chick-fil-A President Says 'God's Judgment' Coming Because of Same-Sex Marriage." *The Christian Post*; "What Dan Cathy Said." *The Atlanta Journal-Constitution*. July 26, 2012.

[6] Blume, K. Allan (July 2, 2012). "'Guilty as charged,' Dan Cathy says of Chick-fil-A's stand on faith." *Biblical Recorder*. North Carolina Baptist State Convention (Cary, NC); Hsu, Tiffany (July 18, 2012). "Is Chick-fil-A anti-gay marriage? 'Guilty as charged,' leader says." *Los Angeles Times*.

[7] Ibid.

[8] http://www.foxnews.com/us/2012/08/15/guard-at-family-research-council-shot; http://www.wjla.com/articles/2012/08/chinatown-shooting-leaves-two-wounded-78851.html.

[9] Starnes, Todd (July 25, 2012). "Rahm: 'Chick-fil-A Values Are Not Chicago Values.'" *Fox News Radio*; Turner, Greg (July 20, 2012). "Mayor Menino on Chick-fil-A: Stuff It." *The Boston Herald*.

[10] http://www.splcenter.org/blog/2010/12/15/splc-responds-to-attack-by-frc-conservative-republicans/.

[11] Interview of Tony Perkins on *Fox News*, August 15, 2012 http://video.foxnews.com/v/1789592747001/family-research-center-president-tony-perkins-speaks-out-following-shooting-points-finger-at-southern-poverty-law-center-for-labeling-frc-a-hate-group/.

[12] *Morning Line with Nic Beres* on Channel 5, WTVF, Nashville, August 2012.

Chapter 2

[13] John 1:1.

[14] We will leave to another day and to another book what it means to be "stupid," "unscientific" and "irrational." Calling those who believe in a Creator names like that is the ad hominem argument some scientists use to keep others from looking honestly at the evidence for a Creator. It is the scientific version of the tactic underlying politics of hate. People don't want to be known as "stupid" any more than they want to be known as "hateful." We will also lay aside for now whether believing the Bible is God's Word is more or less stupid than believing that life on earth came from life on other universes that we don't know about, as some scientists claim.

[15] Take, for example, Christopher Hitchens' statement: "I am not even an atheist so much as an antitheist; I not only maintain that all religions are versions of the same untruth, but I hold that the influence of churches and the effect of religious belief, is positively harmful." http://www.goodreads.com/author/quotes/3956.Christopher_Hitchens?page=2.

[16] "If Christians would really live according to the teachings of Christ, as found in the Bible, all of India would be Christian today." Mahatma Gandhi http://quotationsbook.com/quote/6593/#sthash.muA05OEm.dpuf; "You Christians look after a document containing enough dynamite to blow all civilization to pieces, turn the world upside down and bring peace to a battle-torn planet. But you treat it as though it is nothing more than a piece of literature." Mahatma Gandhi http://www.goodreads.com/quotes/456351-you-christians-look-after-a-document-containing-enough-dynamite-to; In speaking of Jesus and his teachings, Thomas Jefferson

wrote, "A system of morals is presented to us, which, if filled up in the style and spirit of the rich fragments he left us, would be the most perfect and sublime that has ever been taught by man." Letter to Dr. Benjamin Rush, April 21, 1803 in *The Life and Selected Writings of Thomas Jefferson*, Modern Library Edition, Random House, Inc. (1993); "As to Jesus of Nazareth, my opinion of whom you particularly desire, I think the system of morals and his religion, as he left them to us, is the best the world ever saw, or is likely to see." Benjamin Franklin, Letter to Ezra Stiles, March 9, 1790, http://www.beliefnet.com/resourcelib/docs/44/Letter_ from_Benjamin_Franklin_to_Ezra_Stiles_1.html

[17] In regard to whose perception matters, Acts 5:41 is very revealing. We read that Peter and other disciples, after being flogged by the Council, "went on their way from the presence of the Council, rejoicing that they had been considered worthy to suffer shame for His name." Worthy to suffer shame? Those two things, "worth" and "shame," do not go together unless being considered worthy by God was of greater value to them than not being held in shameful regard by those who did not really know God.

[18] Hebrews 5:8.

Chapter 3

[19] It is here that I disagree with Frederick Bastiat who, in his book, *The Law*, says that the power of civil government is the collective power of the individuals who are governed. As is true of civil government, individuals have no power except such as God delegates to them. However, if civil government's power comes from the people (as opposed to from God through the people), then it is hard to reconcile the command that individuals are to leave the execution of wrath and vengeance up to God with the truth that the "ruler" is to exercise the wrath and vengeance of God. Compare Romans 12:19 and 13:4. In these passages it is made clear that there is a scriptural distinction between the power an individual possesses to execute wrath and vengeance as an individual and the power an individual possesses as a governing authority. A person's "power" or "right" to self-defense is not the same as the power to execute God's vengeance on wrongdoers.

[20] John 19:11 (NASB).

[21] Note that the plural word, authorities, is used. There are others to whom God has delegated a measure of this authority such as the family and the church. Therefore, civil government is not the only form of authority on earth. For a more extended discussion of other limitations on the exercise of power by civil government, see chapter 10 and endnote 103.

[22] *See supra* endnote 19.

[23] Daniel 5:30.

[24] King David understood what Nebuchadnezzar did not. In 2 Samuel 5:12 we read this of David: "And David realized that the Lord had established him as King over Israel, and that He had exalted his kingdom for the sake of His people Israel." In other words, David did not see his power as coming from himself. He

also understood that the power given him by God was for "his kingdom," not David's own.

[25] Isaiah 42:8 and 48:11.

[26] Daniel 4:34-35.

Chapter 4

[27] I didn't appreciate it at the time, but my closing statement was a modern contextualization of the Scripture "owe no man anything but to *love, against which there is no law.*" Whether sexual intercourse in all committed loving relationships is biblically ethical is quite a different issue.

[28] Here is a good place to point out that we cannot avoid making truth claims. In fact, the preceding sentence is a truth claim. To deny the existence of truth claims or to deny that we can go through life not making truth claims is itself a truth claim.

[29] "A trustee is a fiduciary of the trust beneficiary. A fiduciary is legally bound to act, within the confines of the law, in the best interests of the beneficiary. A trustee is in a special position of confidence in relation to the beneficiary because the trustee has control of property that is essentially owned by the beneficiary." http://legal-dictionary.thefreedictionary.com/trustee.

[30] John 14:15; 1 John 5:3.

[31] Galatians 2:20.

Chapter 5

[32] A fourth category for the Christian could be "consummation," the wrapping up of history. See, for example, Act 3:21. See also *Creation Regained, Biblical Basics for a Reformational Worldview*, Albert M. Wolters, Pater Noster Press, Wm. B. Eerdmans Publishing Company, (1985).

[33] See Nancy Pearcy, *Total Truth: Liberating Christianity from Its Cultural Captivity* (Crossway Books, First Printing, 2004) page 41.

[34] 333 U.S. 203, 212 (U.S. 1948).

[35] No doubt this provision is a type of religious test for office. But such was not a problem when Tennessee's present constitution was first written in 1870. The prohibition on religious tests in the U.S. Constitution did not apply to the states, but only to the federal government.

Chapter 6

[36] Galatians 5:23.

[37] Romans 3:20.

Chapter 7

[38] *Planned Parenthood of Middle Tennessee v. Sunquist*, 38 S.W.3d 1 (Tenn. 2000).

[39] Leff makes another interesting observation. "I find it enormously interesting that this approach to finding a replacement for a transcendent source of values involves, in effect, a redirection of metaphorical energy: to find a human equivalent for God, there is a focus not on God's goodness, but on His power." God, as revealed in the Bible, provides the philosophical grounding for what men have to grope for once they reject him. It is not surprising, therefore, that politics today, devoid of God, has often been reduced to nothing more than power, measured either by votes, money or weapons.

Chapter 8

[40] Romans 7:7.
[41] Galatians 3:24.
[42] *Planned Parenthood of Southeastern Pennsylvania v. Casey*, 505 US 833, 856 (U.S. 1992).
[43] "Assisted reproductive technologies" means "a range of techniques for manipulating oocytes and sperm to overcome infertility...." http://dictionary.webmd.com/terms/assisted-reproductive-technology.
[44] Since that time, the U.S. Supreme Court has upheld a federal law banning partial birth abortion after earlier holding that a ban was unconstitutional. *Cf Gonzales v. Carhart*, 550 U.S. 124 (U.S. 2007), holding ban constitutional, and *Stenberg v. Carhart*, 530 U.S. 914 (2000), holding ban unconstitutional.
[45] We ought not scoff at the possibility that even in the United States there could some day be a policy requiring forced abortion or forced sterilization with respect to certain people. In 1924, the state of Virginia enacted a law requiring forced sterilization of certain persons, and the law was upheld by the United States Supreme Court in *Buck v. Bell*, 274 U.S. 200 (1927). Here is the court's description of the law:

We have seen more than once that the public welfare may call upon the best citizens for their lives. It would be strange if it could not call upon those who already sap the strength of the State for these lesser sacrifices, often not felt to be such by those concerned, in order to prevent our being swamped with incompetence. It is better for all the world if, instead of waiting to execute degenerate offspring for crime or to let them starve for their imbecility, society can prevent those who are manifestly unfit from continuing their kind. The principle that sustains compulsory vaccination is broad enough to cover cutting the Fallopian tubes. Three generations of imbeciles are enough. *Id.* @ 207.

[46] Matthew 24:12.
[47] Luke 13:34.
[48] First Timothy 2:4.

Chapter 9

[49] Romans 6:6 says the "body of sin," which characterizes who we are without Christ, must be done away with in order for us to no longer be "slaves to sin."

[50] Genesis 3:12.

[51] See, for example, Proverbs 20:4; 21:25, and compare 2 Thessalonians 3:10 to Proverbs 16:26.

[52] Reducing other government spending, for example, on the military, in order to reduce the national debt may be a good idea, but not as a justification for having the money needed to fund welfare programs. The existence of the money to fund such programs does not address the problems of dependency and loss of freedom that those programs create.

Chapter 10

[53] In the first chapter of his book, *On Liberty*, Mr. Mill said there was "one very simple principle" by which to govern society. The only purpose for which the power of civil government "can be rightfully exercised over any member of a civilized community, against his will, is to prevent harm to others."

[54] John Calvin, *Institutes of the Christian Religion*, Book IV, Chapter 20, Section 16, e.g. "Yet we see that amidst this diversity they all tend to the same end. For they all with one mouth declare against those crimes which are condemned by the eternal law of God—viz. murder, theft, adultery, and false witness; though they agree not as to the mode of punishment. This is not necessary, nor even expedient."

[55] So, for example, I have not tried to set forth a theory covering issues like environmental pollution or the private use of land that impairs enjoyment by another of his private land, issues that historically would have fallen more within the sphere of public nuisances or would have been seen as a violation of "public rights." For a discussion of the history of the development of public nuisance law, see Victor E. Schwartz and Phil Goldberg, *The Law of Public Nuisance: Maintaining Rational Boundaries on a Rational Tort*, 45 Washburn L.J. 541 (2006); Richard A. Epstein, *A Conceptual Approach to Zoning: What's Wrong with Euclid*, 5 N.Y.U. Envtl. L.J. 277, 282 (1996).

[56] These first two thoughts are reflected in Proverbs 17:15, "He who justifies the wicked, and he who condemns the righteous, both of them alike are an abomination to the Lord."

[57] Doing wrong that good might result is condemned by Scripture in other contexts as well. In Romans 3:5-8, the apostle Paul notes that our unrighteousness highlights God's righteousness. However, some saw that as an excuse to say that it was okay to sin because it makes God's righteousness seem more glorious. They said, "Let us do evil so that good may come?" Paul's response: "Their condemnation is deserved." In God's sight, the ends do not justify the means.

[58] The tenth commandment prohibiting covetousness is not included because it is an attitude of the heart that, as discussed in the Appendix, the civil law cannot address adequately, notwithstanding our efforts to try to use it for that purpose. However, when covetousness breaks out into actions, such as stealing another person's property, then civil law intervenes.

[59] Deuteronomy 4:6-7.

[60] Understanding this points helps us make sense of Romans 13:5, "Therefore you must be subject, not only because of wrath but also for conscience' sake." People understand the need to be "subject to" the law because of the wrathful consequences of disobedience. But when civil law is grounded in the moral law of God, which was the prevailing view in England and in the early days of America, then Christians need to understand that it also binds our conscience. That also helps explain why, as was said earlier, the magistrate should be careful not to pollute the judgments of God.

[61] In fact, Jesus, in the Sermon on the Mount, points out that the various laws of conduct extrapolated by the Pharisees from the Ten Commandments did not reach the level of the righteousness the law actually required. Jesus was quite clear that, in his eyes, unless a person's righteousness exceeded that of the Pharisees, scrupulous keepers of the letter of the law, then they were not righteous enough to enter the kingdom of heaven.

[62] The affect of the law on our behavior is not different here than the affect previously discussed regarding abortion except that, with abortion, the effect "encouraged" a negative consequence, the devaluation of life and an exaltation of self.

[63] Some would disagree with this idea, arguing that there can be a moral right to do a moral wrong. (For an excellent refutation of this assertion, see Robert P. George, *Making Men Moral, Civil Liberties and Public Morality*, p. 110-128, Oxford University Press, 1993, reprinted 2000). However, the protection of a positive right might *allow* a wrong to be perpetrated. For example, the lawful restriction on the right of civil government to rummage through a person's house without a warrant based on just cause might allow time for critical evidence to be removed. But even here, if removal of the evidence is proved, there has been an obstruction of justice, a crime based on the violation of a victim's right to honesty in the actions of others for the sake of justice being done.

[64] While perhaps most Christians would agree in principle, not all would agree with respect to certain situations. For example, there are Christians who would dispute whether there is a right of self-defense on the ground that it is an assault on the bodily integrity of another that is forbidden because we should simply "turn the other cheek."

[65] This "non-interference" is not a justification for making same-sex marriage legal, but just the opposite. God's nature and character define what is good (His original intention) and, accordingly, they also define the marital relationship. Marriage, for the Christian, is a visible expression of an invisible reality. It is intended to project to a watching world a picture of the diversity, unity, communion, fellowship and complementariness of the Triune God. Same-sex marriage

is inconsistent with the Triune nature of God. One reason is that it substitutes a quality of sameness for the complimentary diversity of the Father, Son and Holy Ghost. Though each person of the Trinity forms one essence, each has a different role or function. Thus, same-sex marriage is not marriage in God's eyes, as it would portray a wrong image of who he is. Thus, for the law to encourage the good, as God defines that term, the law should encourage male-female marriage by not equating it with other human relationships.

[66] It only "may" be a good law because the law could violate some other principle such as failing to recognize the fallenness of man by giving unchecked power to one individual.

[67] For a more detailed application of these general principles, see the Appendix.

[68] See Piper, John, *The Pleasures of God*, p. 237 published by Multnomah Books © 1991, 2000 by Desiring God Foundation. Citing Isaiah 8:12-13, Piper says, "It is a great biblical truth that to fear a thing is to do homage to it....If our lives are guided by the same fears that unbelievers have, then we do not 'regard God as holy.' We do not honor him and revere him as greater than all things. In fact, Isaiah says [Isaiah 51:12-13] it is a kind of pride to be afraid of what man can do while we disregard the promises of God....Fear of man may not feel like pride, but that is what God says it is: 'Who do you think you are to fear man and forget me your Maker.'"

[69] This is not to say that the opinions of constituents should not be considered. Their opinions may, in fact, express a biblical truth that has not been considered or given due weight in the official's evaluation of a proposed law. Nor is it to say that officials should not be wise in discussing an issue or their vote on a piece of legislation. But it is to say that if the official is convinced, before God, that it is the right thing to do, then it should be done. "To him who knows the right thing to do and does not do it, it is sin." James 4:17.

[70] See also Psalm 75:6-7.

[71] John 15:5.

[72] In this particular instance, I acknowledged to the legislator his need to respect those whom God had placed in authority over him relative to the legislative process. But then I shared with him the story of the prophet Jeremiah who kept prophesying "negative things" about Judah's future. In Jeremiah's case, the king's advisors said of him: ""Please, let this man be put to death, for thus he weakens the hands of the men of war who remain in this city, and the hands of all the people, by speaking such words to them. For this man does not seek the welfare of this people, but their harm."(Jeremiah 38:4).

And so Jeremiah was thrown into the muck of a cistern in the prison yard. The question I asked of my legislative friend was whether Jeremiah was being a bad "team player" because his warnings "scared" the "players" on the king's team. The answer was clearly "no" from God's perspective. Jeremiah was faithful to his role on *God's* team, and it is His view of one's effectiveness that ultimately matters.

[73] I had the "pleasure" of an experience in which neither side on a budget issue would move. The task of solving the budget was complicated by the fact that the House and Senate leadership had stacked the committee with people who would only vote one way, in this case, for a personal income tax on wages, which Tennessee did not have. The result was that the fiscal year expired with no new budget and so for several days all but the most vital state services like the prisons, mental health hospitals and highway patrol were shut down.

[74] *Planned Parenthood of Middle Tennessee v. Sundquist*, 38 S.W.3d 1 (Tenn. 2000).

[75] See Isaiah 30:1-3 and 31:1-3 in which Israel is rebuked by God for making an alliance with Egypt for its protection rather than asking God what his plan was. Aligning with Egypt probably looked "reasonable," except for the fact that God had already planned to judge Egypt too.

[76] Some ministers have said that some of the things discussed in this book are too deep for their members or that this "sound bite" world has made it difficult for much sustained thinking among their members. Those concerns may well be valid, but the answer is not to ignore the need but to deal with it. That may mean beginning with smaller, more easily digestible teaching with a view toward preparing people for more "solid food." And certainly, there is nothing wrong with offering more challenging fare in specialized series offered at times other than the Sunday sermon.

[77] I use the word "risk" for lack of a better word. I agree with John Piper's assertion in his book, *Don't Waste Your Life*, that our view of "risk" should be mediated by a firm conviction in our minds regarding the sovereignty of God. *Don't Waste Your Life*, (Crossway Books, 2003).

[78] Ministers afraid of causing offense by being too pointed might get some encouragement by reading Peter's sermon before the Sanhedrin in Acts 4. He was not afraid to point fingers, and thousands were being added to the church! And we cannot forget that Jesus said some things that even his disciples said were "difficult" and hard to "listen to." In fact, because of what he said, many withdrew and stopped following him. (See John 6:60-66.).

[79] I understand that too. I was mindful that not everyone at the law firm in which I first practiced shared my Christian faith. I hate to admit that I never overtly shared my faith with anyone for the intentional purpose of leading them to Christ. Nevertheless, at one point I was told that some of the partners had a concern that "my commitment to my religion and my family" might interfere with my "commitment" to the firm and the practice of law. It was a crucible in which my faith was refined. My wife and I decided I should leave. I truly loved and enjoyed those with whom I practiced law and they were gracious and generous in facilitating my departure but leaving was one of the hardest yet best things that ever happened to me because it set me on my current course.

[80] I know this phraseology will offend many, but I don't think it is biblical to measure a person's inherent dignity or worth by with whom they have sex. The terms that are in vogue right now, to me, reflect an identity bound up in that. In

a sense, I think it is tragic that *anyone* would find their identity in just what they do. We are, in God's sight, more than human doings. So I choose to use a term not laden with identity issues and descriptive of the nature of the act engaged in. For me at least, not confusing actions with identity allows society to discuss the morality of the action without attacking the dignity of the individual as made in the image of God. For the same reason, I almost prefer the term "follower of Jesus" to the term "Christian" as it allows for the baggage associated today with "Christian" to be left aside and allows for a discussion of whether my conduct is consistent with the nature and character of God as revealed in his Word, which was made flesh in Jesus. For a discussion of that baggage, read the survey results found in *UnChristian*, David Kinnaman © David Kinnaman and Fermi Project, published by Baker Books, second printing, December 2007.

[81] Even as I write, these questions come to my mind because I know many Christians will not like what I have written, whether it is biblical or not. Some won't like me because of it and will say "bad things" about me. And it has crossed my mind that if some them are donors, they may no longer support the work I do. So do not read what I have written to imply that I never struggle with these questions. By the grace of God, I pray I will struggle with them less as I mature in the knowledge of God.

[82] I recognize that the way in which we communicate changes and the use of media and technology is not unbiblical. Trusting in them rather than the power of God to do what only God can do—save—is what would be unbiblical. The Hebrews in Jesus' day had their process down to a science, but it did not save them. Refusing to confront sin, as some are prone to do these days, is unbiblical.

Chapter 12

[83] That is the view of law expressed by the United States Supreme Court in *Planned Parenthood of Southeastern Pennsylvania v. Casey*, 505 U.S. 833, 851 (1992): "At the heart of liberty is the right to define one's own concept of existence, of meaning, of the universe, and of the mystery of human life."

[84] In fact, as discussed before, when the focus of law is the individual, to the exclusion of others (often described as the "common good" in legal theory), love grows cold. We may not immediately see the effects of shifting from a theonomistic to an autonomistic basis for law, but the Word of God assures us that, in time, love will grow cold. And a loveless society is not one in which many of us would want to live.

[85] I am using this term as a way to distinguish the institution of the church evidenced by buildings in which worship services and educational programming are held, as distinguished from the church universal of which every believing member is a part.

[86] Acts 1:3.

[87] Psalm 36:9; Colossians 2:2-3.

Chapter 13

[88] Thankfully, the law does not yet make civil disobedience an everyday occurrence, but we are certainly headed that way, particularly if Christians choose to remain silent.

[89] Acts 5:29

[90] It must be kept in mind that Jefferson was writing prior to the U.S. Supreme Court's opinion that the First Amendment should be applied to actions by states. Textually, the First Amendment only applies to acts by Congress.

[91] This was not a reference to some deistic view of law and government, but rather a Christian one. Two of the greatest influences on American legal philosophy at the time were John Locke and William Blackstone. Locke said, "[L]aws human must be made according to the general laws of nature, and without contradiction to any positive law of Scripture, otherwise they are ill made." Locke, *Two Treatises on Government*, Bk II sec 135. (Quoting Hooker's *Ecclesiastical Polity*, 1.iii, § 9) Blackstone, in his treatise, *Commentaries on the Laws of England*, said, "Upon these two foundations, the law of nature and the law of revelation, depend all human laws; that is to say, no human laws should be suffered to contradict these." http://www.constitution.org/tb/tb-1102.htm 1 William Blackstone, *Commentaries* 42 (The University of Chicago Press 1979; Introduction by Stanley N. Katz).

[92] Notes on the State of Virginia.

[93] Note that in this instance Jefferson was acting as a leader of a state, not as leader of the federal government, in keeping with the federalist interpretation previously given the Danbury Baptist letter.

[94] By "one aspect," I am referring to the fact that Jesus fulfilled the role in the Old Testament of prophet, priest and king. The modern church tends to focus on Jesus as our high priest, making atonement for our sins and interceding for us, even as the priests in the Old Testament did. Forgiveness of sin and restoration of a right relationship with God is no doubt a very important part of "God's story." But the modern church has too often forgotten that another part of "God's story" is that God is king over his universe and Jesus is Lord. Jesus will "reign until He puts all His enemies under His feet," at which point he will "hand over the Kingdom to God the Father" so that "God may be all in all." (1 Corinthians 15:24-28.) This is the aspect of God's story that I am addressing in this part of the text.

[95] In Romans 13:4, the magistrate is referred to as a "minister," the word in the original language being "diakonos" from which we get the word "deacon" and by which Paul described his calling in Ephesians 3:7.

[96] The First Great Awakening in the United States started in the 1730s and continued until about 1743. It was commonly seen as a precursor to the War for Independence with England. The Second Great Awakening was a religious revival in the United States that began in the late eighteenth century and lasted until about the middle of the nineteenth century. Its effect was strongest in the Northeast and the Midwest. The Third Great Awakening was in the mid-nineteenth century and lasted into the 1900s. http://en.wikipedia.org/wiki/Great_Awakening.

[97] William J. Federer, *America's God and Country Encyclopedia of Quotations*, FAME Publishing, Inc., 1996, p. 235.

[98] For information about practical ways you and your church can be better informed and more engaged on cultural and governmental issues, contact the author at www.thepoliticsoflovinggod.com.

Appendix

[99] Even those who seek to justify abortion know that killing an innocent person is wrong. But, in their unrighteousness (see Romans 1:18) they deny they have committed murder by redefining a person to exclude a fetus or by denying the innocence of the fetus by calling it a "trespasser," interfering in things like the mother's relationships, education or career.

[100] Genesis 9:5-6. " "Surely for your lifeblood I will demand [a reckoning]; from the hand of every beast I will require it, and from the hand of man. From the hand of every man's brother I will require the life of man. "Whoever sheds man's blood, By man his blood shall be shed; For in the image of God He made man."

[101] It is worth noting that lying is often a way in which the Adamic Shift occurs. A lie often is used to shift blame and responsibility. Thus, if the civil government's policies somehow encourage or do not prohibit lying, it is not taking into consideration man's tendency toward the Adamic Shift.

[102] A natural question might be whose positive rights are being violated such that a lie by a person who is only a witness to an act could be punished for perjury. If the person being interrogated lies in connection with evidence relative to the issue for which he is being questioned, then the positive rights of the parties in the dispute are being violated. Lying to the judge, jury or interrogator is therefore a violation of the positive right to honesty to which those involved in the dispute are entitled.

[103] In discussing the "wrongs" in these examples, it is not my intention to imply that every wrong someone does should be remedied in court or punished by civil government. Even though civil government is to commend good and punish evil, its involvement should be limited by other countervailing considerations. In the present case of lying, every lie should not be cause for punishment by civil government or some kind of judicial remedy. It is for that reason the common law does not recognize lawsuits for lying, only for defamation. By law defamation requires proof of some kind of loss, such as proving that lies about a business resulted in a loss of customers. In other situations, civil government should defer taking action out of respect for other God-established governing authorities such as the family. Civil government should respect the authority and responsibility of parents for the nurture and education of their children. Lastly, prudential considerations can also serve as a limitation. For example, similar to the discussion in endnote 63, civil government could punish more wrongs if it periodically searched every person's house without a warrant, but civil government itself would be disregarding the person's right to private property.

[104] Act 10:34.

[105] We see these three categories in Galatians 3:28, "There is neither Jew nor Greek, there is neither slave nor free, there is neither male nor female; for you are all one in Christ Jesus." The point of the verse is that in the kingdom of God these are false distinctions by which to evaluate a person's worth or dignity before God, and therefore they are false distinctions upon which we should make such judgments. We can see this in Paul's condemnation of Peter's "discrimination" when Peter would not eat with the Gentiles in the presence of Jews. Galatians 2:11-14.

[106] One could argue that the lying neighbor in the preceding example has a positive right to speak that is violated by the law against defamation, but preventing him only from lying does not violate his more general right to speak to others about his neighbor. His right to speak is not destroyed. Taking away a person's right to dispose of his or her property, inherent to the ownership of property, destroys that right.

[107] An easy-to-understand explanation of the fact that property rights are not the same thing as the land and the improvements thereon is found in *Money, Greed, and God: Why Capitalism Is the Solution and Not the Problem*, Jay W. Richards, pp. 94-95 Harper Collins Publishing, 2009, Paperback edition, 2010. According to Richards, the apartment is not "property" because it is an improvement on a piece of land, but because it is "represented by a title that reflects an underlying social reality." That reality is what economist Hernando de Soto says is a lawfully recognized "consensus between people as to how those assets are held, used, and exchanged." Ibid at p. 95, quoting "The Mystery of Capital," *Finance and Development* 38, no. 1 (March 2001).

[108] This is an entirely different situation from those in which the civil government itself is perpetrating the act of wrongful discrimination. The conduct of private actors in their private relationships with one another is fundamentally different from that of civil government's actions against its own citizens. Consider the discussion, *see supra* endnote 19, regarding individuals versus the magistrate expressing God's vengeance and wrath against evil. This understanding is in keeping with the original understanding of our Bill of Rights that served as a limitation on civil government relative to citizens, not as a limitation on the private conduct of citizens toward one another.

[109] *Shelley v. Kraemer, 334 U.S. 1 (1948)* ("Since [the] Civil Rights Cases, the principle has become firmly embedded in our constitutional law that the action inhibited by the first section of the 14th Amendment is only such action as may fairly be said to be that of the States. That Amendment erects no shield against merely private conduct, however discriminatory or wrongful....[The] judicial action in each case [enforcing the restrictive covenant] bears the clear and unmistakable imprimatur of the State." Such deed restrictions should have been made unlawful legislatively by statute as a restriction on the ownership of property. There is now a whole line of cases trying to establish the "criteria" by which state action will be attributed to a private person.

[110] Ignorance of our constitution has also resulted in a failure of people to understand that many laws today regulating actions between private individuals are not based on the protection of some "right" in the Bill of Rights. Rather, they are justified on the ground that the private act affects interstate commerce that, under the U.S. Constitution, Congress has the power to regulate. But, to the average person, this distinction between some "right" being constitutionally "protected" from actions by another person and the actions being prohibited as a regulation of "intrastate commerce" has been lost. To the average person, everything today is about "rights."

[111] First Kings 21.

[112] I use the term "wrongful discrimination" because not all discrimination is wrong, though that has become its accepted meaning in the confused thinking of our day. An employer who employs someone better qualified for a particular job, the person who chooses certain artwork, and the person who refuses to eat "junk food," has "discriminated." The issue isn't discrimination, *per se*, but making judgments based on false or invalid criteria unrelated to the decision at issue. That is why not choosing a person for most jobs because of their skin color would be wrong; it is not a valid criterion related to the job. However, it could be a valid criterion in choosing a person to depict a person of a certain ethnicity in a movie. Choosing an African-American to play the role of Jackie Robinson, who broke the color barrier in professional baseball, is not racial discrimination.

[113] In his Virginia Act for Establishing Religious Freedom, Thomas Jefferson noted that beliefs and matters of opinion are not for the law to act upon. In his words, "it is time enough for the rightful purposes of civil government, for its officers to interfere when principles break out into overt acts against peace and good order."

[114] Herein lies a major problem and fallacy of hate crimes legislation.

[115] When it comes to subsidizing certain businesses and industries, which is nothing more than corporate welfare, the noble goal is to create jobs for people, particularly during tough economic times. Noble goals don't justify wrong means in this situation either.

[116] The application of the principles in this book to the particular situation herein discussed involving the welfare programs run by civil government is not to say that civil government should abruptly stop those programs. I expect some will wrongly attribute those sentiments to me. To me such action would border on dishonesty. Civil government should not hold out a program to people in such a way that some are almost induced into relying on it, and then abruptly leave them in a position in which they may not be able to provide for themselves. But the goal should be for civil government to find ways to return charity to the private sector. To do that, though, every Christian would have to become far more serious about tithing and using his or her blessings to honor God and bless others.

[117] If a government program begins to foster dependence on the government, then the government has undermined personal liberty, not protected and secured it.

And the most well-intentioned charity can also facilitate destructive behaviors by doing things like discouraging thrift and undermining industry.

[118] If there were such a right, then the verses cited in endnote 51 would make no sense. It should also be noted that God did not apportion the same amount of land to each of the 12 tribes of Israel.

Made in the USA
San Bernardino, CA
19 February 2014